PRAY WHILE YOU'RE PREY DEVOTIONS

52 WEEKS OF ENCOURAGEMENT FOR
YOUR SINGLE SEASON

by
Toni L. Wortherly, Esq.

PRAY WHILE YOU'RE PREY DEVOTIONS

52 WEEKS OF ENCOURAGEMENT FOR YOUR SINGLE SEASON

Toni L. Wortherly, Esq.

Printed in the United States of America.

Toni L. Wortherly, Esq.
tonilashaunmusic.com

Cover Art by
Erica Wortherly

10 9 8 7 6 5 4 3 2

This publication is designed to provide accurate and authoritative information with regard to the subject matter covered. It is sold with the understanding that the publisher is not engaged in rendering any professional advice. If legal advice or other expert assistance is required, the services of a competent professional person should be sought.
---From a Declaration of Principles jointly adopted by a Committee of the American Bar Association and a Committee of Publishers and Associations

Pray While You're Prey Devotions

From the book, "Pray While You're Prey: How God Turned my Loneliness and Frustration into Contentment and Commitment," this devotion provides a weekly, year-long uplifting look through Scripture during seasons of singleness, bringing encouragement to you and others while honoring God.

The best way to use this devotion book is to read one devotion at a time, meditate of the Scripture by reading it several times and in different interpretations, saying the prayer, and noting your observations, pertaining to the devotion throughout the week. There are lines for journaling after each devotion or you can keep them in your own personal journal. The most important thing is to focus in on your relationship with Christ and ask God to open the eyes of your heart, so that you can see His plan for your life more clearly. And, if you are in a relationship or begin a new relationship while you are reading, so not stop reading. Ask God to enlighten you on His Will for your relationship as you continue to study His Word in this context.

May God bless you and keep you is my prayer!

DEDICATION

This book is dedicated to Jesus Christ and to single women and men throughout the world who are discovering His kindness, grace and mercy during their time of singleness.

Pray While You're Prey Weekly Devotions for Singles

Week One
A Time to Love

Scripture:
Ecclesiastes 3:8

"There is a time for everything...a time to love..."

Quote from *Pray While You're Prey*:
"...if God desires someone to be in my life, He will not
keep that person from me."

Tick! Tock! Tick! Tock! When I was younger, I did not
really believe that there was such a thing as a
biological clock. I just thought that this concept of
some annoying, nagging urging to settle down, get
married and have babies was mythical in nature.
Then, I turned 30; the age at which I had always
hoped to be happily married and finished having
children. Instead, I was in a failing relationship with
no chance of a baby in sight. That is when the ticking
started. *Tick! Tock! Tick! Tock!*

From the time I was a little girl, I dreamed of being
married. Then, when the possibility that I might never
have the option to give birth to my own children
entered the picture, it was no laughing matter. People
say to me, "You can have a baby anytime you want.
Women are becoming moms all the time all by
themselves." And, that may be fine for other women,
but my babies need a full-time father, and that father
needs to be my husband. So why, I began to think,
won't God send me a husband, with whom I can
have a family?

His reply: *Timing is everything*. We think of time as finite. But God's time is infinite. I know that I have allowed myself to get caught up in timetables, some set up by society and some that were concocted in my own mind. My first marriage was the result of an irrational timetable. I was 21 and unmarried, and I thought that if I didn't get married then, I would be an old maid. Well, I did get married then and I am now, a maid -- not old, but definitely single.

The issue with my logic was that God does not work on timetables. He simply says, "There is a time for *everything*." And, God is so awesome in power that your time to love and my time to love may take place at different times. God knows how to keep track of the perfect timing for every blessing in each and every one of our lives. We have to stay patient and let Him work. I have had many accomplishments that have caused people to be impressed, but I am deeply saddened by all of the times I got in the way of God's timing because I know I missed out on amazing blessings.

God is love. He wants us to know love and feel loved. He wants us to learn how to love His way because that is the only way we can experience the fullness of love towards one another. In a season of singleness, there is a unique opportunity to focus solely on loving God, and as a result, loving God's way. In His timing, everything else will fall into place and it will be worth the wait.

Prayer
Lord, thank You for helping me accept that your
timing is perfect.
Please forgive me for trying to "help" when You
never asked me to.
Lord, teach me how to love Your way while I wait
and when it is my time to love.

In Jesus' Name
Amen.

Reflections for the Week

Read and meditate on this week's Scripture. Say the prayer at the end of the devotion daily and ask for God's wisdom. Write down any revelations or reflections you may have throughout the week.

_____

_____

_____

_____

_____

_____

_____

_____

_____

_____

_____

_____

Pray While You're Prey Weekly Devotions for Singles

Week Two
Bad Boys, Bad Girls, Whatcha Gonna Do?

Scripture:
Proverbs 2:12-15

"Wisdom will save you from the ways of wicked
men, from men whose words are perverse, who have
left the straight paths to walk in dark ways, who
delight in doing wrong and rejoice in the perverseness
of evil, whose paths are crooked and who are devious
in their ways."

Quote from *Pray While You're Prey*:

"They say that love is blind, but if love is blind, then
LUST is a blind, mentally-challenged, deaf mute…"

Why do good girls love bad boys? And, for that
matter, why do good guys want bad girls? What is so
attractive about the person that you know means
nothing, but harm? I would submit that good girls
and good guys do not love bad boys and girls, but
they sure do lust after them. Let's be real, the bad
ones are sexy. I am not talking about those who are a
threat to your well-being; those people should be
avoided at all costs. I am referring to the ones who
are aloof, commitment- phobic, risk-takers; the ones
who only care about what you can do for them, never
giving a thought to what they can do to enhance your
life.

At one point, about thirteen years ago, after a series of failed attempts at relationships, I tried to figure out where I was going wrong. So, I made a list of all the guys that I had dated and looked for their similarities. Once I had that list, I analyzed it to figure out what my red flags should be for my next suitor. But, it wasn't very long before I found myself dating the same exact type of guy again because he was someone to whom I was physically attracted. And, he had that bad boy quality that was so enticing. You know, when you are attracted to someone because they have an "I don't care" attitude, you should probably take the hint and run very far away. So, how do we avoid getting caught in this trap?

Rather than looking through the blinded eyes and deafened ears of lust; we need to seek out wisdom from God. God's wisdom can show us the obvious that we are overlooking, and it can show us layers of someone's personality that are hidden until after you fall in love. How do we get this wisdom? Seek God and meditate on His Word. When I was compiling my list of who not to date, it should have included anyone who does not know God. That is the first red flag for a single, Christian woman or man. We must stop thinking that if we can get someone to fall in love with us; we can make them fall in love with God. We cannot change the hearts of any other person and what usually happens is that the person draws our focus away from God.

God does not want us to be in relationships with bad people. Nor does He want us, in an effort to get them before they get us, to be bad people. He gives us the opportunity to screen those with whom we come in contact by giving us His Word, His wisdom and the Holy Spirit. Our part is to read, understand and listen.

Prayer

Lord, thank You for Your Wisdom.

Thank You for the opportunity to learn what is best for me.

Please forgive me for all of the time that I do not listen to Your warnings.

Please show me anyone in my life that does not belong.

In Jesus' Name
Amen.

Reflections for the Week

Read and meditate on this week's Scripture. Say the
prayer at the end of the devotion daily and ask for
God's wisdom. Write down any revelations or
reflections you may have throughout the week.

_____

_____

_____

_____

_____

_____

_____

_____

_____

_____

_____

_____

_____

Pray While You're Prey Weekly Devotions for Singles

Week Three
No One

Scripture:
Exodus 20:3-6

"You shall have no other gods before me. ...You shall not bow down to them or worship them; for I, the LORD your God, am a jealous God, punishing the children for the sin of the parents to the third and fourth generation of those who hate me, but showing love to a thousand generations of those who love me and keep my commandments."

Quote from *Pray While You're Prey*:

"God doesn't allow us to be in relationships so that we can forget all about him. He is a jealous God. Our focus should be on pleasing Him at all times whether in a relationship or not."

I love music and that will become very obvious throughout these devotions. I do not just love any music; I love music that is creative. I love music that paints a picture in your mind of what the artist is trying to convey. And, I really love music that teaches me a lesson whether it is the intended lesson from the artist or not. Alicia Keys has a song called, "No One." In the chorus, Alicia says, "No one can get in the way of what I feel for you." Now, I am pretty sure she was talking about a relationship with a beau, but imagine if we apply that principle to our relationship with Christ.

No one can get in the way of what I feel for You, Jesus.

It was God's intention all along that we put Him first. When the Israelites received the Ten Commandments from God, putting no one higher than God was right at the top of the list. Not only that, but God was kind enough to explain Himself.

He says, "for I, the LORD your God, am a jealous God." (Exodus 20:5). Now, let's not get this twisted, there is nothing we could possibly have on earth that is better than God, so there is nothing that we love for which He has envy or wishes He had, like we do when we are jealous. I believe God is saying, "I have done so much for you, but you choose to put other things before me or give yourselves and other people the glory for it, and that makes Me angry." And, He let the Israelites know the consequences of that anger in the command; punishment for those who hate Him, and love for those who keep His commands. If you read the Old Testament, you will see that every time God blesses Israel, they shift their focus away to something or someone else, never fully giving God their attention.

I know what you're thinking, *How could they treat God that way*? But, before we go criticizing, we must take a good hard look in the mirror. See, the Israelites were exhibiting this behavior and it was deplorable, but they did not have the 66 books of the Bible like we do. Yet, we often treat God like an afterthought, unless, of course, we need something.

God does not want our focus because He is some brutish, jealous titan. If you take a few moments to recognize God's blessings in your life, how could you not fall in love with Him? He simply wants your love and your focus, so that He can give you the life He has planned for you; your best life. Allow Him to be first always.

Reflections for the Week

Read and meditate on this week's Scripture. Say the
prayer at the end of the devotion daily and ask for
God's wisdom. Write down any revelations or
reflections you may have throughout the week.

_____

_____

_____

_____

_____

_____

_____

_____

_____

_____

_____

_____

Pray While You're Prey Weekly Devotions for Singles

Week Four

Free from Concern

Scripture:
1 Corinthians 7:32-34

I would like you to be free from concern. An unmarried man is concerned about the Lord's affairs—how he can please the Lord. But a married man is concerned about the affairs of this world—how he can please his wife—and his interests are divided. An unmarried woman or virgin is concerned about the Lord's affairs: Her aim is to be devoted to the Lord in both body and spirit. But a married woman is concerned about the affairs of this world—how she can please her husband.

Quote from *Pray While You're Prey*:

"Being single gives us a unique opportunity to grow closer to God."

As Paul put it, the best perk of singleness is freedom from concern. Sure, my ice cream habit stems from a certain freedom from concern about someone judging me for how I choose to consume my food. However, there is a deeper freedom from concern that singleness offers. Married couples, I know because I once was part of one, have to be concerned about each other's pleasure. In fact, I would offer that most marriages break up because of a lack of concern for pleasing one's mate. Think about it. Infidelity, financial problems, and "growing apart" all stem from a certain level of selfishness that really should not be present in a marriage, especially a marriage between two saved, sanctified, Spirit-filled people.

Singleness offers the opportunity not necessarily for selfishness, but for a single-minded focus on living a life that is pleasing to God without concern for what another person might think or say, or, how another person might react. Neither married people nor single people are excluded from keeping focus on God. Nevertheless, Paul recognizes that married couples have to split their focus. Single Christians can be interested in God's voice alone. The only One you have to discuss a major life decision with is God. The only One who you have to listen to is God. The only One you have to honor is God. Your total devotion and attention can be dedicated to God without any concern for a family. Of course, I know that this does not apply to every single person because some people have children. Single parents also have split focus, but I truly cannot speak to that issue as the only thing I have been charged with raising is a very precocious cat.

In any case, every Christian's first focus should be on God. As a single Christian, that focus on God can be our only focus. We can be free from concern, free to move, free to do, free to dream as God pleases.

Prayer

Thank You, Lord for the blessings of singleness.
Please forgive me for complaining about my
singleness
when it is an opportunity to grow closer to You.

Lord, please lead me and guide me on a path that
pleases You.

In Jesus' Name,
Amen

Reflections for the Week

Read and meditate on this week's Scripture. Say the prayer at the end of the devotion daily and ask for God's wisdom. Write down any revelations or reflections you may have throughout the week.

_____

_____

_____

_____

_____

_____

_____

_____

_____

_____

_____

_____

_____

Pray While You're Prey Weekly Devotions for Singles

Week Five
Good Grief

Scripture:
2 Corinthians 1:3-4

Praise be to the God and Father of our Lord Jesus
Christ, the Father of compassion and the God of all
comfort, who comforts us in all our troubles, so that
we can comfort those in any trouble with the comfort
we ourselves receive from God.

Quote from *Pray While You're Prey*:

"As I take this journey to discover what God wants
me to see and do while I am prey, I want to write out
prayers and scriptures that I use to get me through
this experience. I want to remember my thoughts and
meditations, so that my experience may help someone
…. I hope to learn and to teach others…"

I remember, as a child, seeing Charlie Brown in
various unappealing situations like getting picked on
by his friends, being very untalented at athletics, and
just plain being disrespected by a teacher with an
indiscernible language. His reply most of the time
was, "Good grief!"

Those two words seem like quite the oxymoron. How
in the world could grief ever be good? The Bible tells
us that there will be trouble in this world in which we
live temporarily. Not everyone on earth knows God

and not everyone who knows God trusts Him enough to follow Him exclusively. That, my friends, is the perfect recipe for trouble. We all know about the obvious troubles of the world; bad economy, hatred and intolerance, high crime rates and violence. But, what about the troubles and the grief that we face internally? Can grief be good?

It grieves my heart that three of my grandparents will never meet my children. It grieves my heart that I am single, but people throw away perfectly viable relationships all of the time. It grieves my heart that it may not be God's plan for me to ever remarry. It grieves my heart that I know some very lovely people who have not even had a chance to be married. Can grief be good?

Absolutely! When we allow God to comfort our grief, it can become a positive experience. When my grandmother passed away, I did not know that I would ever recover from the level of pain that I felt, but a year later, I found myself comforting people who were going through the same type of loss and feelings of hopelessness.

The same way God comforts us when we are sick, mourning, or have been victimized; He also comforts us through our daily grief, which includes sadness over being single. There is no grief that God cannot handle. As the hymn writer said, "What a

Friend we have in Jesus! *All* our sins and grieves to bear." There is no limit to God's comfort, but when He comforts us, we need to use the comfort we receive to comfort others. This is how we can give Him glory and experience good grief.

Prayer
Thank You, God for being a Comforter.
Please forgive me for holding onto grief instead of
casting my cares upon You.
Lord, please help me use the comfort You give me to
comfort others.

In Jesus' Name,
Amen

Reflections for the Week

Read and meditate on this week's Scripture. Say the prayer at the end of the devotion daily and ask for God's wisdom. Write down any revelations or reflections you may have throughout the week.

_____

_____

_____

_____

_____

_____

_____

_____

_____

_____

_____

_____

Pray While You're Prey Weekly Devotions for Singles

Week Six

Who's Chasing Whom?

Scripture:
Proverbs 18:22

He who finds a wife finds what is good and receives favor from the LORD.

Quote from *Pray While You're Prey*:

"I am the hunted. I should be sought after. As a single Christian woman, I am PREY."

Several years ago, after re-reading Proverbs 18:22, I had the revelation that God's intention was not for me to be constantly seeking the attention and affection of a man. He did not want my time to be consumed with husband-hunting. The only thing I should be desperately seeking for on any given day is more of God. This is not just a word that He spoke to me. He wants us all to live in the natural order of His creation, which means that women should not ever be chasing after men.

So, after many years of setting traps for men, I hung up my hunting gear. I would sit back and wait for "him," whoever he is.

About a year after this declaration, someone found me. I stuck to my guns. He approached me, he called me, and he planned our first date. Everything was going fantastically. Until the day after the first date, when he didn't call after he said he would. So, I called because I thought maybe he had lost my number. When we officially started dating, I made most of the contact and most of the plans, despite my best efforts to wait on him. I had quickly slipped back into chase mode. And, it should come as no surprise that we broke up.

In spite of the good times that we had, the relationship was draining because I was always pursuing and not allowing him the opportunity to pursue me. I was giving a lot of effort and not allowing him the chance to put forth effort. I had disrupted the natural order of relationships. As a result, I am single. In relationships prior to this one, the biblical implications of who should find whom had not really sunk in, but I went into this relationship knowing the right thing to do and still choosing my own way. That is always a recipe for disaster.

This is not about being coy or playing hard to get. This is about being obedient to God. And, when you know better, you must do better because God will not bless disobedience. For the brief time that I was letting him find me, it was exhilarating, but exhilarating quickly turned into exhausting when I stopped listening to God.

God wants us to be in healthy relationships and to be married if that is our desire. God wants our first allegiance to be to Him; however, He is loving and kind and He understands the innate need that many of us have to be with a companion. God created us in such a way that men enjoy pursuit and women enjoy being pursued. Although it may seem like men enjoy being hunted or women enjoy the role of huntress, the Bible clearly states that the man should do the finding. We must obey God's Word to enjoy the

single life and to have great relationships when it is
our time.

Prayer

Thank You, God for giving me an understanding of
Your Word.
Please forgive me for not following Your will in my
relationships.
Lord, please help me to play the role that You
intended for me
to have while single, dating and once I am married.

In Jesus' Name,
Amen

Reflections for the Week

Read and meditate on this week's Scripture. Say the
prayer at the end of the devotion daily and ask for
God's wisdom. Write down any revelations or
reflections you may have throughout the week.

_____

_____

_____

_____

_____

_____

_____

_____

_____

_____

_____

_____

Pray While You're Prey Weekly Devotions for Singles

Week Seven

It Ain't Easy

Scripture:
Matthew 7:14

But small is the gate and narrow the road that leads to life and only a few find it

Quote from *Pray While You're Prey*:

"It's hard enough to be pure and holy when you are alone, but once you meet your hunter, it's even harder."

Olympian Lori "Lolo" Jones made headlines a while ago, and not because she made it to the London Olympics, where she could redeem herself in the 100-meter hurdles, after having fallen while in the lead at the 2008 Beijing Olympics. Lolo was in the headlines on the news, on the radio, on the Internet because she said that staying a virgin is harder than training for the Olympics.

Now, I am not what anyone would consider an athlete; I played three years of sub-par volleyball in eighth through tenth grade and I did win the Presidential Physical Fitness Award in sixth grade, but that is the extent of my athletic ability. When I watch track stars, or any other athlete for that matter, I cannot imagine the level of training that they go through to win races on the national and international levels. So, when she says that it is difficult, but staying pure is even more difficult, you know that staying a virgin is not easy.

Many people wanted to chalk Lolo's virginity up to some training ritual, but she very clearly stated that she does not intend to have sex before marriage because of her relationship with Christ. Now, people want her and Tim Tebow, the world's most famous virgin, to date. I am not really interested in Lolo's potential love life with Timmy, but her love life with Jesus is inspiring.

Staying pure is complicated. It is complicated if you have never had sex. It is complicated when you are in a relationship. It is especially complicated if you have had sex and are trying to live obediently. God is not a cruel god. He is not trying to keep something wonderful and magical from us, but He wants us to enjoy it as married people. God knows the complexities of having a sexual relationship with someone. Those complexities are best handled by people who have committed themselves to each other through marriage. Lolo and Tim get that. It took me a long time, and several slip-ups, but I get it, too.

To know that you are being obedient to God and showing Him that you love Him more than any person on this earth makes purity more precious than an Olympic gold medal or a Super Bowl ring. You might not feel like you are capable of living according to God's Will as it applies to sexual intimacy, but God is able to help you through it. It is one of many narrow doors of Christianity, but the benefits of obedience far outweigh the momentary pleasure of disobedience. No one said it is easy, but it is totally worth it!

Prayer
Thank You, God for giving me the opportunity to
show
You how much I love you by keeping my body pure.
Please forgive me for the times when I have not lived
according to Your Will.
Lord, please help me to be strong enough to refrain
from sex until marriage.

In Jesus' Name,
Amen

Reflections for the Week

Read and meditate on this week's Scripture. Say the prayer at the end of the devotion daily and ask for God's wisdom. Write down any revelations or reflections you may have throughout the week.

_____

_____

_____

_____

_____

_____

_____

_____

_____

_____

_____

_____

Pray While You're Prey Weekly Devotions for Singles

Week Eight

Forgiven

Scripture:
Psalm 103:12

…as far as the east is from the west, so far has he
removed our transgressions from us.

Quote from *Pray While You're Prey*:

"…when you confess your sins and truly repent,
being honest with yourself and with God, He will
forgive you for any and all mistakes…Not only does
He forgive you, but I know that He forgets."

There have been many times that I have thought that
my singleness and childlessness is a punishment for
everything that I have done wrong in my life,
especially concerning relationships. I have felt that
there is no possible way that God would ever give me
the opportunity to marry again because I was
unfaithful during my marriage. I have felt that God
would never give me the opportunity to date again
because I was unable to keep my vow to remain
abstinent in past relationships. I have been tortured
by the thought that I will never have children because,
in a moment of irresponsibility, I prayed that I would

rather never be pregnant than be pregnant at that time.

But, as awful as the mistakes are that I have made, God's forgiveness covers them all. God does not lie. If His Word says, He removes our sins as far as the east is from the west, then that means that He forgives and He forgets. Yes, we still have circumstances in our lives that remind us of our indiscretions, but those circumstances are consequences of disobedience; they are not God's way of lording our failures over us. If we have sincerely asked God for forgiveness, He is faithful in His forgiveness and forgetfulness.

So, why do we dwell on the past and sins that have been erased? For me, I know that the concept is difficult to grasp. It is hard to accept that anyone can love me so much. It is unfathomable that someone cares enough about me to clean up all of the filthy places in my life. I believe we find all of this so incredible because we know that we, in and of ourselves, cannot exhibit this type of love. We struggle to forgive others and to forgive ourselves. Nonetheless, as complex as this kind of love is to understand and display, this is the kind of love that God gives to us and through us, and once we accept that we are forgiven, we can have peace in our lives and move forward.

Now, of course, the devil is beside himself with glee every time we doubt God's forgiveness. Satan wants us to live in the past.

Our past is his greatest weapon because he has no idea what our future holds. Our enemy wants us to feel beaten, broken, and blasphemous. If he can keep us feeling like God cannot love us, then we will not love ourselves. When we do not love ourselves, it is impossible to love others properly. Recognize this lie from the pits of hell and know that you are forgiven. You are loved by God. No one can take that love and forgiveness away.

The only person that God ever said was, "a man after My own heart," was an adulterer and a murderer. This does not mean that sin is acceptable; it does mean that God looks in the heart. And, if we, like David, are truly repentant, God forgives us, forgets the sin, and forms a future for us according to His Will.

Prayer
Thank You, God for Your forgiveness.
Please forgive me for the times that I have sinned and for the times I have refused to forgive those who sin against me.
Lord, please help me to be confident
in the fact that I am forgiven and that You have forgotten.

In Jesus' Name,
Amen

Reflections for the Week

Read and meditate on this week's Scripture. Say the prayer at the end of the devotion daily and ask for God's wisdom. Write down any revelations or reflections you may have throughout the week.

_____

_____

_____

_____

_____

_____

_____

_____

_____

_____

_____

_____

Pray While You're Prey Weekly Devotions for Singles

Week Nine

A Time of Blessing or a Time of Testing?

Scripture:
Ecclesiastes 3:11

He has made everything beautiful in its time. He has also set eternity in the human heart; yet no one can

fathom what God has done from beginning to end.

Quote from *Pray While You're Prey*:

"I want other [singles] to learn that if they will just talk to You, everything will be alright in Your time."

We do not spend our entire life on top of the mountain. There will always be peaks and valleys to life. The reassuring fact for Christian singles is that every situation in our lives is used to for something beautiful. Every time of trial and testing can lead to a time of beauty and blessing.

My pastor once said to me, "Life has ebbs and flows and you can begin to enjoy it as soon as you learn to ride the waves." In order to have peace in our lives, we have to understand that God has a purpose in every season. This season of singleness is not the result of God loving you any less than He loves those whom He has allowed to get married. Singleness can be seen as a time of blessing or a time of testing. The results of this time when we belong to God and God alone will be beautiful.

Being single gives us the opportunity to get to know ourselves and our God more intimately. It is a blessing that allows us to pursue dreams that may not be possible if we had the concerns that come along with having a family. During my time of singleness, I have had the opportunity to see different places in the world. I studied abroad and visited London, Paris, Madrid, and Milan. I have discovered places that I love to visit here in the U.S., like Providence, Rhode Island and Savannah, Georgia. I am not saying that it would not have happened if I had a family. But, there was beauty in being free to discover what the world has to offer.

Being single gives God the opportunity to uncover the places in our lives that we still need to work on before we are in a committed relationship. Singleness is a place where God can test our commitment to Him. He can find out if our focus on Him is because He is the center of our joy or if it is because we have no other options. I have failed this test several times. The fantastic thing about God as a teacher is that He allows retakes on His tests and they are always open book. There is beauty in fixing our flaws before we enter into a relationship with another person.

No matter whether we see singleness as a time of blessing or a time of testing or both, God makes it beautiful. If we take a moment to stop complaining or lusting after things that are not meant for us in this season, we can become content with the plan that God has for us right now. He hears your thoughts and prayers and He knows the desires of your heart. God wants you to experience the most beautiful version of your dreams that is possible, and He will make it so in His time.

Prayer

Thank You, God for being in control of time and every season of my life.
Please forgive me for being impatient as You make everything in my life beautiful.
Lord, please help me to humbly accept everything You are trying to show me in this season.

In Jesus' Name,
Amen

Reflections for the Week

Read and meditate on this week's Scripture. Say the prayer at the end of the devotion daily and ask for God's wisdom. Write down any revelations or reflections you may have throughout the week.

_____

_____

_____

_____

_____

_____

_____

_____

_____

_____

_____

_____

Pray While You're Prey Weekly Devotions for Singles

Week Ten

…Then Why Am I Still Alone?

Scripture:
Genesis 2:18

The LORD God said, "It is not good for the man to
be alone. I will make a helper suitable for him."

Quote from *Pray While You're Prey*:

"We were put on Earth to serve and praise God, but
God knew that man should have a mate or
companion, so he gave Eve to Adam. However, the
gift of Eve did not in any way diminish Adam's duty
to God."

I read it over and over again, "It is not good for man
to be alone…." Those were God's words, not mine.
He knew we would desire companionship, so why am
I still single, Lord? We were created to praise and
please God. We were created in His image, and just as
He loves us, we oftentimes have the desire to love
others. The institution of marriage was ordained by
God from the beginning of time, and yet, I feel left
out because I am still single. Have you ever felt this
way?

In singleness, there seems to be a void. And the void
is only natural, as God said it is not good for us to be
alone. Many single people make it their life's mission
to find something to fill the void left by loneliness.
We vigorously pursue dreams and goals. We invest

time in people and projects. We immerse ourselves in anything we can to avoid the thought of how lonely we feel.

There is nothing wrong with pursuing dreams; it is one of the greatest benefits of singleness. There is nothing wrong with staying busy; it can be helpful to relieve the pain that is sometimes experienced from being alone. However, until we realize that the void we feel can only be filled by God, we will be miserable.

God is the treasure. He is the ice cream and the cherry on top. Sure, being in a relationship is like having a little whipped cream or some slivered almonds or chocolate sauce, whatever you fancy, but the sweetness is found in God alone. Just because God made Eve for Adam it did not mean that Adam was to love, respect or cherish God any less. And, Adam's gift led him astray, as we allow many of the people God gifts us with to do. God wants us to have a suitable helper. But, that helper needs to point us to Christ in times of crisis or confusion.

If you have accepted Christ in your life, you are never alone. Single, maybe. Lonely, sometimes. Alone, never! God is always with us. He is everything we need whenever we need it. Once we realize that, any relationship that God blesses us with will become infinitely more satisfying. We will stop trying to mold our loved ones into the perfect shape to fill our void because the void will be filled by God. How many relationships fail because they are based on our unreasonable and unrealistic expectations of what another person can do for us? Companions are great, but they cannot even begin to compare with being satiated by God alone. If we truly believe in the promises of God, then we know He has a plan for us

and when we are best suited to have our extras, He
will bless us with them.

Prayer

Thank You, God for being all that I will ever need.
Please forgive me for trying to have other people and
pursuits fill a void that only You can fill.

Lord, please help me to be sure of Your promise that
I am never alone
even though I am single and sometimes feel lonely.

In Jesus' Name,
Amen

Reflections for the Week

Read and meditate on this week's Scripture. Say the
prayer at the end of the devotion daily and ask for
God's wisdom. Write down any revelations or
reflections you may have throughout the week.

_____

_____

_____

_____

_____

_____

_____

_____

_____

_____

_____

_____

_____

_____

Pray While You're Prey Weekly Devotions for Singles

Week Eleven

Treasured

Scripture:
Proverbs 31:10-30

A wife of noble character who can find? She is worth
far more than rubies. …Charm is deceptive, and
beauty is fleeting; but a woman who fears the LORD
is to be praised.

Quote from *Pray While You're Prey*:

"Who can find a good, righteous, worthy, honorable,
moral, upright, honest woman? I know that a man
who is listening to God could find her. Who can be a
good, righteous, worthy, honorable, moral, upright,
honest woman? Any woman who is sincerely living
her life for Christ will fit this description…if [we]
follow Christ's example and believe in God, [we are]
invaluable treasures."

There are many people who have told me that I am
intimidating. The people usually cite my educational
background or level of ambition. However, I do not
pursue me dreams because I want others to feel
inferior to my accomplishments. I pursue goals
because when I read Proverbs 31, it tells a story of a
woman who is bold and hard-working, selfless and
ambitious, and that woman is described as an
invaluable jewel. That woman is revered as someone
to be praised, not feared. That is the kind of woman I

want to be. That is the kind of woman that all Christian women should strive to be. That is the kind of woman a Christian man should desire.

So many times, we get caught up in the superficial qualities of people. Now, don't get me wrong, everybody has their own checklist and non-negotiables, but when we meet someone that fits that checklist, we need to make sure that we are not just focusing on the outer man or woman, but also on the person's character. Is this person a whole person in Christ? Is this person waiting for a man or woman to fill her or his every need? Does this person trust in God to fulfill his or her life? Can this person be supportive of the dreams that God has placed on your heart or will they be jealous or intimidated by your drive and success?

I believe that God created us, men and women, to be compatible with one another. In many ways, we need each other, but we can survive apart from one another. In fact, we can do more than survive, even while we are alone; we can thrive. The only One we need to make us whole and complete is God. So, why not seek to be whole in Him and pursue the dreams He places in our hearts as a single person? Then, when God allows a man to find that woman of noble character, the man should be grateful for a woman with qualities that will never fade. When God pushes a woman to be her best, she should be thankful that He has built her into a woman whose value is far above rubies.

The inner strength that God builds in us is the trait that often gets overlooked. We sometimes forget that charm and beauty fade, not just on women, but on men as well. Single saints with a true heart and passion for the Lord are to be treasured. You are treasured by God; you should accept nothing less than that from anyone else. Live a life filled with character and reverence to God and everything else will fall into place in due season.

Prayer

Thank You, God for giving me dreams and passions
to pursue.
Please forgive me for waiting for someone else
to make me feel whole when I am made whole only
by You.
Lord, please help me to know and remember my
worth, **to** only allow myself to be treasured,
and to recognize the treasures that surround me.

In Jesus' Name,
Amen

Reflections for the Week

Read and meditate on this week's Scripture. Say the prayer at the end of the devotion daily and ask for God's wisdom. Write down any revelations or reflections you may have throughout the week.

_____

_____

_____

_____

_____

_____

_____

_____

_____

_____

_____

_____

Pray While You're Prey Weekly Devotions for Singles

Week Twelve

Looking Around

Scripture:
Psalms 37:7- 11

Be still before the LORD and wait patiently for him;
do not fret when people succeed in their ways, when
they carry out their wicked schemes. Refrain from
anger and turn from wrath; do not fret —it leads only
to evil. For those who are evil will be destroyed, but
those who hope in the LORD will inherit the land. A
little while, and the wicked will be no more; though
you look for them, they will not be found. But the
meek will inherit the land and enjoy peace and
prosperity.

Quote from *Pray While You're Prey*:

"We need to trust in God or trust in our own eyes; we
can't have it both ways."

One of the most dangerous things a single Christian
can do is start looking around at other single people,
especially those that are not Christians. Inevitably, it
will seem as though we are doing everything right, but
remain single while they are doing everything wrong
and are dating and happy. Looking around at other
people's lives is detrimental to your spiritual walk, so
do not do it. The devil knows this weapon of mass

destruction. He will whisper in your ear every time you look at another person who has what you believe you want and try to convince you that God is holding out on you.

Here are some examples: you go out with friends, dressed in an appealing, but modest way. Your smile catches the attention of some men, but every time you look around, the men are dancing, flirting, or talking with a girl who is not leaving anything to the imagination. You start to think, "What gives? I am presenting myself in an appropriate way. I am not being overtly sexual, but I am also not a prude. Why don't I get any attention?"

For the guys, you engage a woman in intelligent conversation. You make her laugh and maybe you even compliment her. But, you see her desperately pursuing a guy who talks down to her and grabs her backside. You start to think, "Is being a respectful guy even worth it? Why do nice guys finish last?"

In all honesty, are these really the people we want in our lives? Hopefully, the answer is no. If not, you may want to take some time and pray about that. God knows what is best for us. I know that it seems like we are doing *everything* right (although, there is always room for improvement) and remain single. Meanwhile, others are drinking heavily, having casual sex, and just being plain wrong, but they get to be a part of a couple. But the happiness that those who behave wickedly seem to be enjoying is fleeting. The joy of the obedient Christian is eternal.

While it may look like the wicked are prospering and the wise are suffering, consider that there would be far worse suffering if we chose the path of the wicked over patiently waiting on God. Do not get caught up in looking around at other people. Be content with what God has given you in this moment, knowing that He cares for you and knows what is best for you. It matters not whether those behaving badly are happy. That is between them and God. What truly matters is that we trust God enough to believe in His promises for our lives and not to focus on others.

Prayer

Thank You, God for being faithful and trustworthy.
Please forgive me for being envious of what others have, especially when they are not living in obedience to You.
Lord, please help me to be still, steadfast and content knowing that You know what is best for me and when to add it to my life.
In Jesus' Name,

Amen

Reflections for the Week

Read and meditate on this week's Scripture. Say the
prayer at the end of the devotion daily and ask for
God's wisdom. Write down any revelations or
reflections you may have throughout the week.

_____

_____

_____

_____

_____

_____

_____

_____

_____

_____

_____

_____

_____

Pray While You're Prey Weekly Devotions for Singles

Week Thirteen

Focus

Scripture:
Matthew 14:29-31

Then Peter got down out of the boat, walked on the
water and came toward Jesus. But when he saw the
wind, he was afraid and, beginning to sink, cried out,
"Lord, save me!" Immediately Jesus reached out his
hand and caught him. "You of little faith," he said,
"why did you doubt?"

Quote from *Pray While You're Prey*:

"God doesn't want us to be alone if we desire not to
be. But any time that you put anyone or anything
before God, it is a sin and displeasing to God. God
will not bless anything that is displeasing to him."

Peter is by far my favorite disciple. He is so fiery and
ready to fight for what he believes in, even when he is
wrong. Peter is passionate. You can tell he loved Jesus
sincerely, even after he denied knowing Christ, his
disappointment in himself shows that he was truly
brokenhearted that he had not stood up for his
Savior, his Friend.

One of my favorite Peter moments is walking on the
water. I was not there, so I do not know what was
actually said by other people on the boat, but I can
only imagine, based on my knowledge of human

nature what the other passengers were thinking. Some probably thought Peter was very brave. Others probably thought he was a show-off. And, oh, when he started to sink! I can just hear it now, "Where's your big faith now, Peter?" Or, "Mmm hmm, you thought you were all big and bad, Peter, now look at you. You're going to drown!"

Why didn't Peter just keep his eyes on Jesus? It could have saved him a lot of trouble and embarrassment. I have to ask myself that question more often than I like. Why can't I just stay focused on Jesus? I was abstinent for over years. It started as a bargain with God (which we should never do, but I was young and foolish), but then, I began to see how much more clearly I saw the world when I was not living in constant disobedience. Being single was still difficult for me, but not unbearable. Then, I met someone, and it only took a few months before I stopped focusing on what God wanted for my life and started focusing on making the relationship work. I began to sink back into my old habits, rather than trusting God to heal the relationship or to end the relationship because it was not His best for me. I was drowning!

When we sink into disobedience, it will start to feel as if God is further and further away from us, but He has not moved. It is our focus that has shifted and caused the distance. But then, God says, "Why do you doubt Me?" God has brought me through too much for me to lack faith in Him. He has also shown me how much better my life is when I live in obedience to His Word.

The best part of the story is that Jesus stretched out His hand and caught Peter. He said, "You of little faith." This indicated that Peter had some faith. And, if we can just have a little faith, even after we start sinking, God will not let us drown. He will catch us, correct us, and come closer to us as we draw nigh to Him. If being single is not what you desire for your life, it can be difficult, but keep your focus on God.

Prayer
Thank You, God for always catching me before
I drown due to my own lack faith.
Please forgive me for being disobedient and losing
focus.
Lord, please help me to never doubt You or Your
love for me.

In Jesus' Name,
Amen

Reflections for the Week

Read and meditate on this week's Scripture. Say the prayer at the end of the devotion daily and ask for God's wisdom. Write down any revelations or reflections you may have throughout the week.

_____

_____

_____

_____

_____

_____

_____

_____

_____

_____

_____

_____

Pray While You're Prey Weekly Devotions for Singles

Week Fourteen

Then I Saw A Rainbow

Scripture:
Isaiah 41:10

So do not fear, for I am with you; do not be
dismayed, for I am your God. I will strengthen you
and help you; I will uphold you with my righteous
right hand.

Quote from *Pray While You're Prey*:

"Don't ever miss out on your blessings worrying
about what someone else has. You have too much to
be grateful for. If a blessing is meant for you, you will
have it when God is ready to give it to you."

Some days are better than others. I thank God that I
can go for weeks, sometimes months without feeling
lonely. But, occasionally, it happens. Usually, when
other circumstances in my life are not going the way I
want them to go, I start lamenting that I would not
even care about these other circumstances if I had a
relationship. If I had a relationship, then I would have
the support I need to pursue my dreams. Maybe, if I
had a relationship, I would not even have the same
dreams and none of it would matter.

One morning on the way to church, which is usually
when the devil tries to get all up in my ear, I was just

feeling down. Though I know it is not true, I felt like no one really cared about me. I tried to listen to music and sing, which almost always makes me feel better, but it didn't work. This was just going to be one of those funky days. I would get to church, plaster a fake smile on my face, worship, and then, go home and feel sorry for myself.

In the midst of my pity party, I felt a prompting to look in the rearview mirror, and then, I saw a rainbow. Rainbows are a symbol of God's covenant that He would never flood the Earth again; they are also a sign to me that God is sovereign and has everything under control, even when the flood waters of life start to rise. Immediately, I felt better. I knew that I did not have to worry about anything that was going on in my life. God has everything under control.

Not only does He have everything under control, but He knows what He is doing. He knows what we need and when we need it. So, we can make ourselves miserable by looking around at what other people have or we can praise God for what we have. Anything, any blessing under the sun that is meant for me, will be mine in God's appointed time. The same goes for you. Yet, we waste so much time and energy doubting that God has our best interests in mind.

God is with us all the time. He will give us the strength we need to get through the tough times. And, when we can no longer carry the weight, He will hold us up. He will carry us and help us. There is no need to worry or fear or be dismayed if God is your God. Will we feel down sometimes? Absolutely; just don't stay down. Think of the rainbow, God's promise that He is in control. Then, pick yourself up and enjoy living the life that He has given you.

Prayer

Thank You, God for being in complete control over
my life and every circumstance.
Please forgive me for worrying when things don't go
my way.
Lord, please help me to see the rainbow,
the promise of your power, in every situation in my
life.

In Jesus' Name,
Amen

Reflections for the Week

Read and meditate on this week's Scripture. Say the prayer at the end of the devotion daily and ask for God's wisdom. Write down any revelations or reflections you may have throughout the week.

_____

_____

_____

_____

_____

_____

_____

_____

_____

_____

_____

_____

_____

Pray While You're Prey Weekly Devotions for Singles

Week Fifteen

God is NOT a Genie

Scripture:
Mark 11:24

Therefore I tell you, whatever you ask for in prayer, believe that you have received it, and it will be yours.

Quote from *Pray While You're Prey*:

"I have no problem asking God for what I want because His word says that I can. If there is something he doesn't want to give me, He will say 'no.'"

If you found a lamp, rubbed it, and a genie popped out saying, "I will grant you three wishes," what would you wish for? Many people answer that question with, "more wishes!" Some people would wish for money, some would wish for fame, some, especially if they are reading this, might wish for a loving spouse. I would love to be all holier-than-thou and say that I would wish for world peace or something selfless, but I know me better than that.

It is okay to fantasize about what you would wish for with your magical wishes; however, too many of us treat God like He is a genie. We treat him as if He is responsible for giving us our every desire. All we have to do it name it and claim it or blab it and grab it.

God is NOT a genie. Yes, God wants us to come to Him with our every desire. But, God also wants us to be so in tune with Him that His desires for our lives become our desires.

A genie lives in a bottle. He is summoned out when someone rubs the lamp, and then, he grants the wishes and goes back to the lamp. Can you imagine what this world would be like if God was limited to only acting upon our selfish whims? I do not even want to think about it. What if God was confined to a small lamp? The God I serve is way too big for that!

Still, we read verses like Mark 11:24 and misinterpret it to mean that we can just make our three wishes, believe with all of our hearts, God will say the magic words and then our desire will appear. That is not how it works. If that were the case, yours truly would not be single and childless. We can absolutely ask God for whatever we desire, but we need to understand that if it is not in His Will, He will say "no."

When Jesus asked God to spare Him from the crucifixion, God said, "no." Notice what Jesus prayed, though, He said, "Nevertheless, not My will, but Thy will be done." That is the part we forget. We ask God for a myriad of people, places and things to come into our lives, but we give no thought to the fact that God wants us to live our best life; the life that will bring Him glory. Ask, seek, and knock; the Word of God says you can. Just be sure that you are asking for more of God, seeking His face and knocking on doors of opportunity to be more like Him. Then, you will have everything you desire and even more than you could ever imagine.

Prayer

Thank You, God for hearing my prayers of
supplication.
Please forgive me for being selfish when I make
requests to You.
Lord, please help me to know the desires You have
for my life
and to request that which will draw me closer to You.
In Jesus' Name,

Amen

Reflections for the Week

Read and meditate on this week's Scripture. Say the prayer at the end of the devotion daily and ask for God's wisdom. Write down any revelations or reflections you may have throughout the week.

_____

_____

_____

_____

_____

_____

_____

_____

_____

_____

_____

_____

Week Sixteen
The Art of Giving

Scripture:
Proverbs 18:16

A gift opens the way and ushers the giver into the presence of the great.

Quote from *Pray While You're Prey*:

"Be a gift in his life, not a burden."

What is the purpose of being in a relationship? God concluded very early on that it was not good for man to be alone (Genesis 2), so He made a helpmeet for Adam. Since then, we have been surrounded by relationships of all kinds: spouses, significant others, children, siblings, friends, and co-workers. Our lives are generally filled with all types of relationships. So, what is our purpose in being in a relationship?

When I first looked at Proverbs 18:16, I was thinking about how I could prepare myself to be a great mate for someone. I needed to work on my control issues and my neediness. I wanted to be a gift to someone, and not a burden. This principle can apply to all of the relationships in our lives, including the most important one--the relationship with Christ. When we give the gifts of love and friendship freely, we not only add to the lives of those to whom we are giving, but we add to our own lives as well.

There is no greater feeling that giving to meet the needs in someone else's life. Not giving because of what you will receive in return or because of a sense of obligation, but freely giving your time, talents and treasures to be a blessing to someone else. When I am having a bad day, even if I do not always feel like it, I try to think of something that I can do for someone else. I am not trying to score brownie points with God. But, if I can be a blessing in someone else's life, it takes my focus off of problems and points me towards praise.

One of our functions in any relationship is to be a gift. Even while we are single, we can be a gift to our families and friends. No one wants to continue a relationship with someone who is constantly bringing them down. I want someone to come into my life who will add to it. When people ask me about how I feel about being single and waiting for the right person, I let them know, "I have the cake; I am waiting for the icing!" As a matter of fact, God has used this season in my life to prune and mature me so much that sometimes I feel like I have the cake and the icing, and I am just waiting for my ice cream.

Sometimes, we approach relationships with a selfish agenda. I believe selfishness is at the center of every failed relationship. Right now, is the time to ask God to use what He has already blessed you with to help others and to work on those parts of you that may cause someone else to feel burdened.

If we focus more on being a gift, rather than receiving gifts, not only will we find our relationships are more fulfilling, we will find our lives to be more fulfilling.

Prayer

Thank You, God for every resource that You have
given me, so that I can be a gift to others.
Please forgive me for putting so much emphasis on
what others can do for me
and not using Your gifts properly.
Lord, please help me to see the needs of others
that I can fulfill and to live unselfishly in my
relationships.

In Jesus' Name,
Amen

Reflections for the Week

Read and meditate on this week's Scripture. Say the
prayer at the end of the devotion daily and ask for
God's wisdom. Write down any revelations or
reflections you may have throughout the week.

_____

_____

_____

_____

_____

_____

_____

_____

_____

_____

_____

_____

_____

Week Seventeen

The Green-Eyed Monster

Scripture: Exodus 20:17

"You shall not covet your neighbor's house. You shall not covet your neighbor's wife, or his male or female servant, his ox or donkey, or anything that belongs to your neighbor."

Quote from *Pray While You're Prey*:

"We shouldn't even think about what God has given someone else other than to thank Him for blessing that person. And if the person is not of God, we really shouldn't care about her earthly possessions because our reward is in Heaven."

So, there I was minding my own business in the lounge at my law school, when a classmate and so-called friend of mine burst in the room in a huff. "What's the matter?" I asked. "I hate you," she replied. I thought for sure that she was kidding, but she wasn't. She began to berate me for having a husband, good grades and an active social life. She admitted, on more than one occasion, that she was jealous of me. If there was ever a clear depiction of exactly what the Bible tells us not to do in Exodus

20:17, this was it. Most of us aren't as bold as this sister because we envy in secret.

Now, before we go on getting all holier- than- thou about this sister's attitude, we need to check ourselves. There have been MANY times when I have felt the same way, but just didn't say it. What she didn't know and later came to realize was that my marriage was failing and studying and having a social life were an escape for me. I learned a couple of things from this situation, though. First, jealousy often blinds us to the truth. Second, it's called the green-eyed monster because a monster is exactly what envy turns us into.

For me, the root of jealousy is not that I am unhappy for the person who is being blessed. I am jealous because I do not know when or how my blessing will come to pass. I get jealous because it seems that everything is going so well for other people, and I am trying to live the right kind of life, yet not getting the desires of my heart.

So, how do we fix this envy problem? First, stop looking around. Stop fixating on what others have. I mean, this was one of the original Ten for a reason. Second, stop looking down. We must stop looking down on others when they are blessed and stop looking down on ourselves when we do not get what we want when we want it. Finally, start looking up. Look to God for peace and patience, not possessions. He has already given us more than we deserve and He owes us nothing. Yet, He is still merciful and gracious and will provide our every need. We either believe that or we don't.

So, if we know that God will provide our every need, there is no reason to be jealous of anyone else. I have had people jealous of me (at least they were according to my mom) and I have been the jealous one. The only One with a right to be jealous is God because He is the only One who has invested enough in us to have our full, undivided attention. The green-eyed monster needs to go away for good; it is not a good look for anyone, but especially for a Christian.

Prayer

Thank You, God for providing all of my needs according to Your riches in glory.
Please forgive me for being jealous of what others have.
Lord, please help me to stay in my lane and focus on You.

In Jesus' Name,
Amen

Reflections for the Week

Read and meditate on this week's Scripture. Say the prayer at the end of the devotion daily and ask for God's wisdom. Write down any revelations or reflections you may have throughout the week.

_____

_____

_____

_____

_____

_____

_____

_____

_____

_____

_____

_____

_____

Pray While You're Prey Weekly Devotions for Singles

Week Eighteen

Where's Your Head At?

Scripture:
Matthew 6:21
"Where your treasure is, there your thoughts will also be…"

Quote from *Pray While You're Prey*:

"Before any hunt begins and before there is any capture, single[s] need to focus on their relationship with God."

It is amazing how our thoughts can hold us captive when we are instructed to take our thoughts captive (2 Corinthians 10:5). On more than one occasion, I have found myself mindlessly watching television and everything that happens on any show I immediately relate back to the situation with which I am struggling. Usually, that situation is singleness. I find myself daydreaming about my future family. In times when everything is quiet, I think about how much I yearn for a loving husband and children of my own.

Perhaps these thoughts crowd my mind because that is where my treasure lies in those moments. At those times, I want nothing more for my life than to have this picture perfect ideal family fantasy. And, there is nothing wrong with desiring to be in a family unit. God created family. The problem arises when we stop just thinking casually about these desires and begin to fixate on the desires.

There is a problem when our focus is shifted from God to our desires. There are so many verses in the Bible about guarding our thoughts. Thoughts can lead to actions. And, depending on what our thoughts are, those actions may be disobedient to God. That is why we are instructed to think on true, honorable, just, pure, lovely, good, virtuous, and praiseworthy things (Philippians 4:8). If we are thinking about these things, then the actions that follow cannot help but be pleasing to Him.

The things that we spend the most time thinking about show God what we truly treasure. The most dangerous thoughts are ones about issues or people that seem benign. I am not talking about illicit sexual thoughts, hateful thoughts, or destructive thoughts. I am speaking of thoughts about family, friendships, and finances. I am talking about the thoughts that start off in a good place in your heart, but end up being used by the devil to cause you to doubt God.

The devil will take the thing that you desire most and ask, "Why hasn't God sent you a husband yet?" Or, "Why won't God give you that job you have been working so hard for?" The devil will make you think that God has been holding out on you.

He has been using the same trick since the beginning of humankind. It still works. Why stop now?

We must realize that God is the ultimate treasure. I am not saying that every thought we have is going to be about God; I do not know anyone who can do that. However, God and His ways and His will should be the only thoughts on which we fixate. Living the life that He has planned should captivate our thoughts. Our relationship with God should be our only obsession.

Prayer

Thank You, God for being the greatest treasure.
Please forgive me for thinking too hard about other things
that distract me from living the life You have for me.
Lord, please help me to keep my focus in the right direction.

In Jesus' Name,
Amen

Reflections for the Week

Read and meditate on this week's Scripture. Say the
prayer at the end of the devotion daily and ask for
God's wisdom. Write down any revelations or
reflections you may have throughout the week.

_____

_____

_____

_____

_____

_____

_____

_____

_____

_____

_____

_____

_____

Pray While You're Prey Weekly Devotions for Singles

Week Nineteen

The Inside Scoop

Scripture:
Psalm 25:14

The LORD confides in those who fear Him; He makes His covenant known to them.

Quote from *Pray While You're Prey*:

"Fear of God is the key to His secrets. I do not speak of fear in the sense of being scared, but in the sense of reverence and respect."

I have made so many mistakes in judgment when it comes to character that one day I said, "Okay, God, I need You to put a force field around me, so that no one who is not good for me can get to me. And then, when the right one comes along, I need You to put a big, bright, neon sign (like "Eat at Joe's") over his head. I had lost faith in my ability to make right decisions. That lack of confidence in my relationship decisions spilled over into every other decision in my life.

In the beginning, my disdain for the prospect of making bad decisions was paralyzing. I literally was not willing to make any moves because I feared that I might make the wrong move and end up headed in the wrong direction and knocking myself further off-course. However, eventually, I realized that I had someone better to trust than myself: God. My miscues led me to put *all* of my trust in Him. And, not just in the major things like jobs, relationships, money; in EVERYTHING.

I fear the Lord. I am not scared of God (although, I am glad to be living in the age of grace--have you read the Old Testament?); I reverence God. I respect God. I have learned that God knows what is best for me and that He has a future plan for me and a right now plan for me that will work out for my good if I will listen to Him and obey His voice.

I have to believe that as I continue to show reverence for God, whether in quiet time or by simply being obedient to His leading, He will reveal anything that I need to know to me. That is the beauty of the God we serve. Anything that He is not showing us, He is holding back for a good reason. That gives me hope as I wait for my spouse to come into my life. I am not being obedient to get answers or to get what I want. If that were the case, I would have stopped being obedient when I felt God was saying 'no' and 'wait' too much. I am being obedient because I respectfully fear the Lord and His greatness. I know that He is stronger and wiser than I will ever comprehend. So, I will wait patiently for His secrets to my life to be revealed.

Prayer

Thank You, God for loving me enough to not give
me any information that I will misuse.
Please forgive me for not being respectful to You in
my actions and in the way I divide up my time.
Lord, please help me to listen, move when necessary
and be still when necessary.

In Jesus' Name,
Amen

Reflections for the Week

Read and meditate on this week's Scripture. Say the
prayer at the end of the devotion daily and ask for
God's wisdom. Write down any revelations or
reflections you may have throughout the week.

_____

_____

_____

_____

_____

_____

_____

_____

_____

_____

_____

_____

Pray While You're Prey Weekly Devotions for Singles

Week Twenty

How do I Know I am Saved?

Scripture:
John 14:26

But the Advocate, the Holy Spirit, whom the Father
will send in my name, will teach you all things and will
remind you of everything I have said to you.

Quote from *Pray While You're Prey*:

"I am not saying that I am never lonely, but I know that
the world could be devoid of all human life, except me
and

God would still be here with me."

I think some people might expect to see fireworks.
You know, you walk down the aisle, you pray, you
confess, you ask Jesus into your life and then, you feel
changed, but you don't really see any physical
manifestation of salvation. So, how do you know you
are saved? I used to struggle this question. I knew that
I had confessed God, but because of my sinful nature
and my humanness, I wondered if I was really saved.

It was not an all-of -a-sudden, glitter falls from the
sky, and I start glowing kind of change that people
could see. As a matter of fact, I am not sure if anyone
else noticed. Nonetheless, over time I felt more free

to be who God wants me to be regardless of what anyone else thinks about it. That is what it feels like to be saved. That is what the indwelling of the Holy Spirit feels like.

And, the Holy Spirit only resides in you if you are saved.

So, why I am talking about this in devotions about being single? Because nothing that I say will ever help you if the first relationship in your life is not intact. Sure, there are plenty of unsaved people in happy relationships. If I wanted to right now, I could go find someone to be happy with, but that is not good enough for me. I want the kind of relationship that God has set aside for His children. And, in order to have that, I must first be fulfilled by a relationship with Christ, so that I am not putting unreasonable expectations on my future mate.

If you can still do the sinful things that you have always done and it never bothers you; you might want to check your salvation. If you can still go to the same places you know you have no business going to and it does not bother you; you should probably check your salvation. If you can hear people talk about God, Jesus or the Holy Spirit disrespectfully and it does not bother you, you might want to check your salvation. We are not perfect. Notice I said, "it does not bother you."

Sometimes, we will make mistakes and fall back into old behaviors, but it should grieve our spirit. If it does not, we may need to have a reality check about whether or not the Holy Spirit really resides there.

Our dedication to our relationship with God, our first love, will determine how well our relationships work with other like-minded saints of God. And, an added bonus of salvation is knowing that no matter what your relationship status is, you can know that you are NEVER alone!

Prayer

Thank You, God for the comfort and guidance of the Holy Spirit.
Please forgive me for all of the times when I do not listen to the prompting of the Holy Spirit.
Lord, please help me understand that I will not lose my salvation,
but I can lose my joy when I am not obedient to Your leading.

In Jesus' Name,
Amen

Reflections for the Week

Read and meditate on this week's Scripture. Say the prayer at the end of the devotion daily and ask for God's wisdom. Write down any revelations or reflections you may have throughout the week.

_____

_____

_____

_____

_____

_____

_____

_____

_____

_____

_____

_____

_____

Pray While You're Prey Weekly Devotions for Singles

Week Twenty One

At War

Scripture:
Galatians 5:17

For the flesh desires what is contrary to the Spirit, and
the Spirit what is contrary to the flesh. They are in
conflict with each other, so that you are not to do
whatever you want.

Quote from *Pray While You're Prey*:

"the Bible says, we will have battles between the Spirit
and our flesh constantly."

There is a Cherokee legend called two wolves that
says:

An old Cherokee is teaching his grandson about life.
"A fight is going on inside me," he said to the boy.

"It is a terrible fight and it is between two wolves.
One is evil - he is anger, envy, sorrow, regret, greed,
arrogance, self-pity, guilt, resentment, inferiority, lies,
false pride, superiority, and ego." He continued, "The
other is good - he is joy, peace, love, hope, serenity,
humility, kindness, benevolence, empathy, generosity,
truth, compassion, and faith. The same fight is going
on inside you - and inside every other person, too."

The grandson thought about it for a minute and then asked his grandfather, "Which wolf will win?"

The old Cherokee simply replied, "The one you feed."

As Christians, we can apply this principle to the spirit and the flesh. The Bible warns us that they will constantly be in conflict. The spirit wants to live in obedience and the joy of salvation; the flesh wants to live in opulence and the justification of sin.

The battle is not always over something huge like whether to pray or to party or whether to shout to the Lord or give a shout out to your favorite booty call. Some battles take place deep within and are more subtle. For example, I often experience the battle for peace of mind. The spirit wants to be content with what I have. The spirit knows that God is in control and that He has a plan for me. The flesh wants to focus on what I do not have, and sometimes, what others have. The flesh wants me to feel that God has abandoned me; that He has left me alone.

When these battles rage on, I often end up in tears. The tears are expressions of pain for the fact that I have allowed so much nonsense to enter into my flesh, through my eyes and my ears, that it sometimes feel like the flesh is just kicking the mess out of my spirit. I get upset because I know that I read enough and pray enough to know that the devil is a liar and God is on the throne. Still, when it comes to the singleness, the childlessness, the loneliness, I oftentimes let the flesh get the upper hand.

So, what is the solution? The solution is to seek God's face and rely on the Holy Spirit to give comfort as promised.

The solution is to focus on the promises kept by God and the promises to be kept by God rather than focus on the plight of singleness. As the story suggests, the solution is to feed the spirit and to starve the flesh.

Prayer

Thank You, God for the promise that You alone are God.
Please forgive me for feeding my flesh more than my spirit.
Lord, please help me to focus on your faithfulness and allow my spirit to win the battles and the war.

In Jesus' Name,
Amen

Reflections for the Week

Read and meditate on this week's Scripture. Say the
prayer at the end of the devotion daily and ask for
God's wisdom. Write down any revelations or
reflections you may have throughout the week.

_____

_____

_____

_____

_____

_____

_____

_____

_____

_____

_____

_____

Pray While You're Prey Weekly Devotions for Singles

Week Twenty Two

Never-ending Conversation

Scripture:
1 Thessalonians 5:17

…pray continually

Quote from *Pray While You're Prey*:
"I had many talks with God. I am a pray-without-ceasing kind of girl. I came to understand what that meant during this particular time in my life."

At some point in my life, I realized that what I deemed to be me just talking to myself was not me talking to myself at all. It was prayer. Prior to this point, I felt that in order to pray, I had to get on my knees, bow my head, and close my eyes. Or, I felt I had to lay prostrate before Him to get His attention. But, as my pastor often says prayer is not about a position. Whether I am driving in my car, sitting in my classroom, on my couch in my living, in the mall, in church, in bed, it does not matter, I can pray all of the time. And, thank God for that!

When the Bible says to pray without ceasing, I used to think that it was impossible. Then, I got in touch with my inner dialogue and I discovered that the things I was saying, thinking, and asking were not things for which I had answers. The only One who could calm my innermost fears or answer my deeply thought-out questions was God Himself. So, I realized that prayer is a conversation. It is the constant conversation that I have with Christ. It is the time when I stop to praise Him for the sunshine that pokes through on a rainy day. It is the time when I am taken aback by the fact that He loves me, and I did nothing to deserve it. It is the time when my mind wanders into place it has no business going and I ask for forgiveness. It is the times when I have questions and I ask the all-knowing Father.

Without constant communication between God and I, there is no telling how many more mistakes I would have made in my life. I have already made plenty trying to be a big girl and do things on my own. There were many times when I refused to talk to God about something because I didn't want to know His answer. It is the same way we pick and choose which friends to go to for advice. It seems more comforting to hear what we want to hear, but in communication with God, He wants us to hear what we need to hear.

In the single season, depending on how social a creature one is, there is a lot of time spent alone. That time can be dark and depressing or it can be peaceful and productive. One way to enjoy the "me" time that God has blessed us with is to communicate with Him and to listen to find out what the best use of our time will be. How can we be vessels for God in this season? How can we allow Him alone to be our comfort and our all? God will answer these questions and many others, but we have to talk to Him. We must have a never-ending conversation.

Prayer

Thank You, God for being a God who will allow me
to speak to Him
and will answer me when I have questions.
Please forgive me for seeking to communicate with
others before I seek You.
Lord, please help me to listen and never be afraid
to come to You with praises, confessions and
concerns.

In Jesus' Name,
Amen

Reflections for the Week

Read and meditate on this week's Scripture. Say the
prayer at the end of the devotion daily and ask for
God's wisdom. Write down any revelations or
reflections you may have throughout the week.

_____

_____

_____

_____

_____

_____

_____

_____

_____

_____

_____

_____

_____

Pray While You're Prey Weekly Devotions for Singles

Week Twenty Three

Being Single Will Not Kill You

Scripture:
Psalm 118:17

I will not die but live, and will proclaim what the
LORD has done.

Quote from *Pray While You're Prey*:

"I honestly believe that loneliness is one of the devil's
favorite weapons. In my life, there hasn't been a more
powerful weapon."

They (the proverbial 'they' of whom no one really
knows the identity) say, "What doesn't kill you makes
you stronger." It is kind of a rallying cry for the
stormy times of life. It is the comfort in knowing that
a trial might take you to the brink of death, but on the
other side of it, you will be better, wiser, stronger, and
able to face even more challenges of life. I don't know
about anyone else, but there have been times when
my life felt like loneliness itself would kill me. It did
not feel like it would make me stronger at all. It felt
like I was getting weaker and weaker by the moment.

There was even a time in my life when I considered
hurting myself, so that those I loved would have to

surround. The possibility of death seemed, but a mere inconvenience to my plan. I felt that if I succeeded the loneliness would end because I would be surrounded by people who cared about my life. And, if the plan took a left turn and I did not survive, I would never feel the pain of loneliness again. I am well aware of how irrational that line of thinking was, but at the time, I was so depressed that it actually made sense.

Even though, God had shown me in that instance that all I needed to know is that He is there for me, caring for me, and that He has my best interest in mind, there are still times when it feels like being single is going to be the end of me. But, every time that happens, I survive. What's more is that I survive with a testimony.

As the psalmist wrote, I realize that I will not die but live. Furthermore, I live to proclaim that being single will not kill you. It may seem like it will at times, but those are the times when we must press in to Jesus' loving arms a little more. The times when no one will answer the phone, or no one seems to be available to lend a shoulder on which to cry are the times in my life when I have experienced the most intimacy with my Savior, God. They are the times when I know He is there. They are the times that confirm that where my strength ends, His strength begins.

It is okay to cry out to God in your loneliness. Even Jesus cried out to Him in His darkest hour. It does not mean that you will no longer be single, but He will give you what you need to feel able to keep pushing forward in the life that He has planned out for you. It will be a life that is full of more than you could imagine; a life that will bring glory to His name. You will live and not die.

Prayer

Thank You, God for showing me that being single
will not kill me even when I think it will.
Please forgive me for allowing my loneliness to make
me think irrationally
about how much You love and care for me.
Lord, please help me to understand the purpose of
this season
and to live in that purpose for Your glory.

In Jesus' Name,
Amen

Reflections for the Week

Read and meditate on this week's Scripture. Say the
prayer at the end of the devotion daily and ask for
God's wisdom. Write down any revelations or
reflections you may have throughout the week.

_____

_____

_____

_____

_____

_____

_____

_____

_____

_____

_____

_____

Pray While You're Prey Weekly Devotions for Singles

Week Twenty Four

One Day I Stopped Asking

Scripture:
Isaiah 40:31

…but those who hope in the LORD will renew their strength. They will soar on wings like eagles; they will run and not grow weary, they will walk and not be faint.

Quote from *Pray While You're Prey*:

"…if [we] will just talk to You, everything will be alright in Your time."

It seems like I have been thinking about not being single from the day I hit preschool. I still remember my first little crush at the daycare center. We chased each other around the playground, giggled and laughed with each other all day. I just always felt like I was not meant to be alone. Fortunately, I was nearly an adult when I made the choice to disobey God and give away my virginity. That decision caused some pain and anguish, but not nearly as much as it would have if it had happened earlier in my life.

While that decision was a bad one and it strained my relationship with God, I, eventually, got on the right track. I knew that I wanted to be married. So, I prayed and prayed that God would send me a husband. And, I thought He did. After all, I met my ex-husband at church. Nevertheless, I realized that my decision to marry Him was a huge mistake. I was not waiting on the Lord so much as I was just waiting on someone to be willing to marry me.

After my marriage, I still wanted to be married; forever married. So, I kept asking and asking. And, I met someone with whom I thought I would spend the rest of my life. I asked God, correction, I begged God to let him ask me to marry him. That never happened, and the relationship ended. I was crushed. At that point, I just wanted God to make the hurt go away. So, I started talking to Him and I started listening to Him. And, I am not sure when it happened, but one day, I stopped asking.

It had been part of my prayers for so long, "And, Lord, please send me a boyfriend…a husband…someone to love me like you love me." I had felt like once I had a mate, my life would be complete, but after spending time just communing with God, I finally realized that, with Him, my life is already complete. I didn't have to ask anymore. All I had to do was waiting. And, in my waiting, He would strengthen me. Yes, there would be times when singleness would test my limits, but not to the point of disobeying God and trying to get Him to do my will.

I started asking God what He wants for me. And, I learned how to wait. I do not always like waiting, but I have been waiting for so long, and I have been blessed so heartily in the midst of my waiting, that it seems silly not to continue. We must know and trust that God knows and wants what is best for us. I still ask God for things, even occasionally for a mate, but it is no longer my number one prayer. And, I have certainly learned to wait for His answers to all prayers.

Prayer

Thank You, God for the wisdom to know that You know what and who is best for me.
Please forgive me for trying to answer my own prayers rather than waiting on You.
Lord, please help me to remember to ask that Your Will be done in my life, not mine.

In Jesus' Name,
Amen

Reflections for the Week

Read and meditate on this week's Scripture. Say the
prayer at the end of the devotion daily and ask for
God's wisdom. Write down any revelations or
reflections you may have throughout the week.

_____

_____

_____

_____

_____

_____

_____

_____

_____

_____

_____

_____

Pray While You're Prey Weekly Devotions for Singles

Week Twenty Five

Masterpiece

Scripture:

Galatians 5:25-26

Since this is the kind of life we have chosen, the life of the Spirit, let us make sure that we do not just hold it as an idea in our heads or a sentiment in our hearts, but work out its implications in every detail of our lives. That means we will not compare ourselves with each other as if one of us were better and another worse. We have far more interesting things to do with our lives. Each of us is an original.

Quote from *Pray While You're Prey*:

"I am working for God and myself, not wearing myself out for someone else. That may sound selfish, but if you're single, this is the time for a little selfishness. You always keep God first, and He will make sure that you are not crossing the line between being a little selfish and totally self-centered. So, use your "me time.""

Every artist hopes to create a masterpiece; that one original work that will no doubt make the world stand still and notice. It is a work so original that no one will dare compare it with any other because there is nothing of its kind. It stands alone and is taken just for its own beauty, its own decadence, and its own wonder. No matter the medium every artist tries over and over again until he or she has finally made the piece of work that defines his or her talent. And, an artist is fortunate if he or she has one masterpiece, but some of the greatest creative minds have more than one.

God, the ultimate Creator, has many masterpieces; too many to number. Anyone who finds his or her fulfillment in living the life that God has for him or her is one of His masterpieces. As such, as the Scripture suggests, each of us is an original. There is no comparing my life to your life. There is no time for that. There is time, however, to explore every intricate detail of ever unique quality that God has given you…especially, if you are single.

God has sewn each of us together in such a particular way that when we tap into the greatness for which He has called us, we can be an amazing asset to this world and more importantly to the Kingdom of God. However, we get so caught up in what others are doing, what gifts they have, what talents they possess, or what people surround them, that we downplay how marvelous God has made us.

We must stop comparing. If we choose to live a life led by the Spirit and really work every detail of our lives according to His plan, then we have to trust that He has given us what we need in every moment of every day of our lives. We must not yield to the temptation to say that another of God's masterpieces is greater or has it better because they have something that we desire. We must focus on our own mission, our own imprint in this world, and the impact on society that God has chosen for us. The season of singleness gives ample opportunity for this exploration.

Much like we would not compare works of Picasso to those of Beethoven because they are completely different genres, we cannot compare ourselves to another Christian, or non- Christian for that matter, and say that God may one more special than the other. God knows every one of our capabilities and vulnerabilities and He is able to use it all for His glory. He can take each of us and make a masterpiece if we will surrender and only compare ourselves to the example of Christ, and not other people.

Prayer

Thank You, God for making me an original.
Thank You for having a specific plan for my life.
Please forgive me for comparing my life to the lives of others.
Please forgive me for downplaying your ability to make me into a masterpiece.
Lord, please help me to focus on being the person that you need me to be.

In Jesus' Name,
Amen

Reflections for the Week

Read and meditate on this week's Scripture. Say the
prayer at the end of the devotion daily and ask for
God's wisdom. Write down any revelations or
reflections you may have throughout the week.

_____

_____

_____

_____

_____

_____

_____

_____

_____

_____

_____

_____

Pray While You're Prey Weekly Devotions for Singles

Week Twenty Six

The Workout

Scripture:
Philippians 4:13

I can do all this through Him who gives me strength.

Quote from *Pray While You're Prey*:

"There are times when we need to be all by ourselves, so that God can get through to us. I am still learning to accept that."

I have never really been an athletic person. I love watching sports, but the fact that I hate sweating pretty much hinders any actual playing of sports. I have come up with pretty much every excuse in the world as to why I do not work out. I have gone through different weight cycles in my life. First, I was a stick figure until I was about 22. Then, I got married and gained about 20 pounds. Then, I got divorced and I lost 185 pounds (that's a joke; you can laugh). Every time I gained weight again, it got more and more difficult to lose it and keep it off. Eventually, I just decided on an acceptable weight and I figured out ways to stay as close to that weight as possible.

Emotional fitness seems to be a little trickier. I have had three really big breakups, and, just like my weight cycles, each time a major relationship ended, it was more and more difficult to bounce back. I have discovered, though, that emotional strength and physical strength are both byproducts of what you take in and how you exert your energy. When I spent all of my energy just trying to find the next mate, it was exhausting. There were times when I thought I would never survive being single.

However, when I started getting a daily diet of God's Word and started focusing my energy on using the gifts He had given me, I started to feel stronger and stronger. I still have some down days, but those are the days when I need to do a little more intense workout; I need to pray more, read more, listen more. I have read Philippians 4:13 all of my life, but in my seasons of singleness, it has had more relevance to me than in any other times. Where I am weak, God is strong, so as I continue to use His Word and prayer to emotionally and spiritually workout, He gives me the strength I need to make it through each day. He helps me to not focus on singleness, but on the work He would have me do for the Kingdom.

Just like I don't care to sweat in a physical workout because it makes me feel yucky and gross, there are times when I don't feel like being alone and I am mad because I feel yucky and gross, but being alone is exactly where God needs me to be, so that I can live my best life. He needs my focus and attention, so that I can be fruitful and fulfill His purpose for my life. So, He will give me all the tools I need, if I will use them, to gain the strength it takes to keep pressing. And, He will do the same for you if you will allow Him to lead your emotional and spiritual workout.

Prayer

Thank You, God for accepting me as Your own,
and as such, giving me everything I need to survive.
Please forgive me for paying more attention to what
others think I should have or what I think I need.
Lord, please help me to listen to Your voice
and to engage in emotional and spiritual workouts
when I am feeling weak.

In Jesus' Name,
Amen

Reflections for the Week

Read and meditate on this week's Scripture. Say the
prayer at the end of the devotion daily and ask for
God's wisdom. Write down any revelations or
reflections you may have throughout the week.

_____

_____

_____

_____

_____

_____

_____

_____

_____

_____

_____

_____

Pray While You're Prey Weekly Devotions for Singles

Week Twenty Seven

Control

Scripture:
1 Thessalonians 4:3-5

It is God's will that you should be sanctified: that you
should avoid sexual immorality; that each of you
should learn to control your own body in a way that is
holy and honorable, not in passionate lust like the
pagans, who do not know God

Quote from *Pray While You're Prey*:

"If you want an instant self-image booster, stop
giving away pieces of yourself to potential mates."

When I was younger, I love Janet Jackson's music.
The first song I remember getting down to was
"Control."

When I was 17, I did what people told me
Did what my father said and let my mother mold me

But, that was long ago...I'm in control!

The song came out well before I was seventeen, but
oddly enough, when I was seventeen, I made a choice
that would change my life completely. Now, I had
vowed to God to remain pure until I was married.

God had helped me out by not allowing me to have a real boyfriend until I was nearly an adult. But now, I was in a relationship that I knew would last forever and we were committed to each other; we just couldn't get married because of school, so it was almost like we were married…just not on paper.

It's amazing, as I write it now, it seems like a completely irrational justification for sin, but then, I think I truly believed it. I think I really believed that going to get married and being married were the same thing, so I broke my vow to God to stay pure. I put my relationship with my beau before my relationship with Christ because I was in CONTROL!

Clearly, because I am writing this devotion series for singles, that relationship did not last forever. It took a while for me to regain control over my physical urges, which led to too many ill-advised relationships (one is too many, so don't sit there and try to figure out a number). Why? Well, even though I was in control of my decisions, I clearly did not have control over lust and trust.

The lust part is self- explanatory. But, when it comes down to it, I did not trust God. When I finally met someone with whom I could see forever, I did not want him to leave me. Had I trusted God, I would have placed the relationship in His hands and said, "Lord, Thy will be done." But, I could not take the risk that His will was for me to be alone again, so I blatantly disobeyed God's will in order to keep my man.

Again, obviously, that did not work out too well because I am writing this devotion. Call me old-fashioned, but I do not think that men and women realize the spiritual impact of sex. We know the physical impact. We can most times calculate the emotional impact, but there is a spiritual impact as well that seems to be ignored. For me, submitting to the lust of the flesh caused significant spiritual damage. I did not think that God would or could love me again, but I am so glad that I was wrong. Not only does He love me, but now I have truly placed Him in control because the only way for me to control my body is with His help and His guidance. Abstinence is not impossible with God. Surrender control to Him and He will help you through this time of singleness and temptation.

Prayer

Thank You, God for being willing to take control over my life.
Please forgive me for thinking that I could handle physical urges and passionate lust on my own.
Lord, please help me to be wise enough to avoid compromising situations and to trust that You know what and who is best for me.

In Jesus' Name,
Amen

Reflections for the Week

Read and meditate on this week's Scripture. Say the
prayer at the end of the devotion daily and ask for
God's wisdom. Write down any revelations or
reflections you may have throughout the week.

_____

_____

_____

_____

_____

_____

_____

_____

_____

_____

_____

_____

Pray While You're Prey Weekly Devotions for Singles

Week Twenty Eight

Lost Keys Faith

Scripture:
Psalm 131:3

…put your hope in the LORD both now and
forevermore.

Quote from *Pray While You're Prey*:

"By faith, I believe that the [mate] with my desires will
be made known to me, and you should believe that as
well."

It was a normal day off from work, and I planned to
go grocery shopping with my mom. I made three
more stops and grabbed lunch before I headed home.
I pulled in the garage, reached for my keys, which I
naturally and subconsciously almost always throw in
the cup holder, but they weren't there.

I had no worries. I knew the keys had to be in the car,
so I unloaded my bags, ate my lunch, watched some
television, and then, I remembered that I had never
looked for my keys. First, I felt a tiny bit of paranoia
because my name is on two of my key chains, so I
didn't want an unwelcome guest at my house. Then, I
thought about an order that I had coming in the mail,
so

I needed the mailbox key. So, I went on about my day and when I got home, I started searching again. I still found nothing, but my car is really clean.

I went to bed, said my prayers and asked God to show me the keys. I woke, and I started reading the devotions for the day.

One was about resting in God. The other was about being specific in prayer. So, I prayed again. I said, "Lord, I am trying to feel safe, even though, there is a small chance that someone could break into my house, but I know You will protect me. Can you please show me where the keys are?" Then, I realized I hadn't emptied all of my shopping bags. I threw open the cabinet door and pulled down the first bag I saw, but no keys. I looked up and saw another bag, as I pulled it from the shelf, I heard my keys jingling. I started jumping and shouting and dancing.

So, what is the point of all of this? I have read and heard of mustard-seed faith, but I never really understood the concept. How could faith so small, a tiny glimmer of hope, yield results? I found out that mustard-seed faith is a lot like lost keys faith. It is holding on to the minute bit of hope that you have left that there is Something greater and Someone bigger than anything your eyes can see.

How does that apply to singleness? Well, there is nothing in my life right now that indicates that I will ever have another relationship or that I will have the children and family I desire. Nevertheless, I cling to the little hope that I have that God does not mean for me to be alone and, in His appointed time, I will have the desires of my heart because He promised me that. By the way, I often try to figure out why things happen the way they do, and I truly believe I went through this just so that I could write this devotion. So, whether it is mustard-seed faith or lost-keys faith, never let go of it. You will not ever regret believing that God can change your situation!

Prayer

Thank You, God for showing me what just a little faith can do.
Please forgive me for every time that I have doubted that You are able to come through for me.
Lord, please help me to quiet the voice of unbelief and to cling to my faith in every situation and circumstance.

In Jesus' Name,
Amen

Reflections for the Week

Read and meditate on this week's Scripture. Say the prayer at the end of the devotion daily and ask for God's wisdom. Write down any revelations or reflections you may have throughout the week.

_____

_____

_____

_____

_____

_____

_____

_____

_____

_____

_____

_____

_____

Week Twenty Nine

Father Knows Best

Scripture:
1 Samuel 22:20-21, 25

God's way is perfect. All the LORD's promises prove true. He is a shield for all who look to Him for protection.

Quote from *Pray While You're Prey*:

"…once we stop fighting our singleness, we can grow much closer to God."

One thing I have learned about children is that it is very difficult to stop them when they are determined to do something, even if the something that they are determined to do is dangerous. Some of us might resort to reverse psychology to try to get the children in our lives to do what we actually want them to do. Let's face it, children, especially those of the teenage variety, would rather do anything other than what you want them to do.

I am actually not sure who is harder to stop from harming themselves, teenagers or toddlers. Have you ever tried to hold a three-year-old down that was determined to get away? The squiggle and squirm and scream. They know how to make their little bodies into dead weight, which makes them super difficult to hold on to, and the minute you let them go, they will do whatever it is that you told them not to do.

As much as children can be difficult to corral, we older human beings are not exactly a walk in the park. I am so glad that I am not God. He clearly and plainly tells us what to do and what not to do, and like rambunctious toddlers or rebellious teenagers, we choose to do life our way. It is as if we are saying, "Lord, I don't think You know what You're talking about. I have a better plan."

Rather than accepting where God has us in our lives and praising Him for all that He has given us, we start squirming and squiggling and screaming, trying to get out of His grip. What we fail to realize is that the tight grip He has on us is there to protect us.

I cannot speak for anyone else, but this I know, God can and will do EVERYTHING He says He will do. God's way is the best way. If I want His protection, He will be my shield. But, I, like many others seem to forget this when I am having a fit of rebelliousness or just plain having a fit. I try to fight everything that God is doing in my life instead of just pressing in to Him and resting in Him knowing that He has everything under control.

How many things have you tried to do on your own that came out perfectly? I can think of none. We have a loving Father who promises life more abundantly if we will just live His way. He is so loving that He still takes us back after we try to live without Him. The truth of the matter is that we either trust Him or we don't. I pray that each day we choose to trust in His promises because the Father knows best.

Prayer

Thank You, God for protecting me, even when it
means protecting me from me.
Please forgive me for not trusting that you know best.
Lord, please help me to accept where you have
me and when I get squirmy, squeeze me tight and
don't let go.

In Jesus' Name,
Amen

Reflections for the Week

Read and meditate on this week's Scripture. Say the prayer at the end of the devotion daily and ask for God's wisdom. Write down any revelations or reflections you may have throughout the week.

_____

_____

_____

_____

_____

_____

_____

_____

_____

_____

_____

_____

_____

Week Thirty

Adjustments

Scripture:
Luke 8:48

Then He said to her, "Daughter, your faith has healed
you. Go in peace."

Quote from *Pray While You're Prey*:

"Convert your passion for being [married] into a
passion for a stronger relationship with Christ, and
you cannot go wrong."

One summer, at the end of the school year, I treated
myself to a massage. The massage therapist was going
through her checklist of questions and asked me
about back pain. I told her that I had been
experiencing a lot of back pain for several months.
She did her best with my massage and I felt a great
deal of relief and relaxation, but she recommended
that I see a chiropractor because she said something
did not feel right.

I followed the advice of my massage therapist and
made an appointment at the chiropractor. He showed
me that I had been compensating for a genetic
ailment and it resulted in several bones being out of
alignment. Nearly every health problem that I had

that year, including, back pain, knee pain and headaches, could be traced to my spine being out of alignment. The doctor recommended physical therapy.

It occurred to me recently that this episode with my back was not unlike how I approached my singleness. When I was first divorced, I compensated for being single by going out with people I had no business dating, but after a while, I cleaned that part of my life up and started building my relationship with God. So, I forgot that I had a propensity toward making bad relationship choices when I entered into my next relationship. Getting over that break up was more miserable than any other breakup.

I became extremely negative about the prospect of having a successful relationship or even marriage. Some people made comments about my singleness, but no one is a harsher critic of me than me. I would say that I want to be in a relationship, but if I am truthful, I did not really believe it would happen. I thought I was too damaged, too undeserving to be loved. Then, it occurred to me that I needed to make some adjustments. I needed to adjust my spiritual walk and find satisfaction in Christ Jesus. And, I needed to adjust my thought life; I needed to stop doubting that God could send me the exact person for whom I have been waiting.

Just like the chiropractic adjustments, I need to make a blatant effort to make these adjustments daily until they become a natural part of my routine. Then, as they become more natural, I may only have to make an adjustment every once in a while, when I am really in pain and I need more than what comes naturally. The point is that we have to make a choice each day to be positive and full of faith. God has proven that

He is faithful and able. We must adjust our thoughts and believe.

Prayer

Thank You, God for helping me make adjustments to my spiritual walk and thought life.
Please forgive me for being overtly and subconsciously negative about what you can do in my life.
Lord, please help me to stay positive and help my unbelief.

In Jesus' Name,
Amen

Reflections for the Week

Read and meditate on this week's Scripture. Say the
prayer at the end of the devotion daily and ask for
God's wisdom. Write down any revelations or
reflections you may have throughout the week.

_____

_____

_____

_____

_____

_____

_____

_____

_____

_____

_____

_____

Week Thirty One

Who Says You're Not Good Enough

Scripture:
Romans 5:8

But God demonstrates his own love for us in this:
While we were still sinners, Christ died for us.

Quote from *Pray While You're Prey*:

"I have had the occasion to think that I was the
bottom of the barrel. I wasn't pretty enough; I was
book-smart, but not street smart enough; I just
wasn't…enough."

People who know me now would never know that,
for more of my life, I struggled with self-esteem
issues. If I am being honest, when I look back at my
relationship mistakes and failures, many of them
stemmed from the fact that I undervalued myself.

I made up for feeling inadequate by trying to
outperform and out-achieve others. My parents made
every effort to tell me how great I was and that I
could do anything. Unfortunately, their praise and pep
talks were drowned out by all of the negativity that
perceived was coming from my peers. When I got
older, and out of my very long awkward phase, the
pendulum swung in the completely opposite

direction. I went right past self-esteem into pure, unadulterated conceit. I was pretty and I felt pretty and people (meaning guys) started to notice. But, that inner awkward girl was ill -prepared to handle the attention gained by her cocky counterpart. I did whatever I needed to do to keep the attention because I thrived on getting attention.

It wasn't until recently that I discovered that the only One I truly need love from is my Heavenly Father. He is the only one that I should be working and living for, and not so He can give me praise, but at a testimony of praise back to Him for all He has done in my life.

The reality is that, regardless of what we look like, how smart we are, how accomplished we may be, God, the Father, knew that spiritually, we were not good enough to receive His love. And yet, while we were still not good enough, He sent His Son, Jesus Christ, as a sacrifice for our sins to unite us with Him. He does this so that those who believe in Him can be good enough and live lives that are more than enough through Him, here on Earth and for eternity in Heaven. If He loved us that much, when we really were not good enough, who is anyone else to say that once we are His, we are not good enough? Is there really anyone's opinion that matters more to you than God's? Who said you were not good enough? Family? Friend? Enemy? You?

Well, I have news for you, friend, God says, "You might be all messed up, but I sent My Son to clean you up before you even asked or accepted it, and I offered it because I love you." You don't have to get better, live better, or do better before you come to Christ. He accepts us as we are and heals and delivers us into being better. No one who claims to love you

should ever make you feel that you are not good
enough, including yourself. God does not lie, and He
said that you were good enough to love when He
sacrificed His Only Son.

Prayer
Thank You, God for loving me
before I knew how to love You or even love myself.
Please forgive me for placing the opinions of others
higher than Your opinion of me.
Lord, please help me to know that I am loved and
lovable despite what my circumstances look like.

In Jesus' Name,
Amen

Reflections for the Week

Read and meditate on this week's Scripture. Say the prayer at the end of the devotion daily and ask for God's wisdom. Write down any revelations or reflections you may have throughout the week.

_____

_____

_____

_____

_____

_____

_____

_____

_____

_____

_____

_____

Pray While You're Prey Weekly Devotions for Singles

Week Thirty Two

All We Need Is Love

Scripture:
1 John 5:2-3

This is how we know that we love the children of
God: by loving God and carrying out his commands.
In fact, this is love for God: to keep His commands.
And His commands are not burdensome...

Quote from *Pray While You're Prey*:

"If you don't love God's people, then you don't love
God. If you profess to be a child of God, then you
are one of

His people that you have to love."

I try to get out of the house every once in a while, just
to be sure that I don't become a complete hermit.
Sometimes, it is easier than other times to be in public
by myself. Most times, I am perfectly comfortable
getting a meal or even watching a movie alone. Being
alone is a part of my life and I have grown to value
this time of singleness. Then, there are the times
when being out in public by myself is terrifying and
painful. Fortunately, those times are not nearly as
often as the enjoyable times, but when they come

around, I have found that I need to take a deep breath and get back to the basics.

What are the basics? I have to remember that the key to fulfilling my purpose here on earth is obedience to God. In fact, that is how I show God I love Him. I mean, let's face it; there is NOTHING I can give to God. He owns the Universe. All He ever asked us for was love. He commanded that we love Him above anyone or anything. And that love is shown when we obey Him and love His children.

Many people make living this life so much more complicated than it has to be when all we have to do is love. This is not about romantic love. This is about something much deeper. This is the kind of love that causes you to take a leap of faith even though you are scared out of your mind. This is the kind of love that makes you show compassion and mercy towards people who are malicious and hateful towards you. This is the kind of love that makes you look in the mirror each day and shout praises for being fearfully and wonderfully made. All we need is love.

We do not need some magic formula. We do not need a conference or convention. We do not need a strategic, hook-up plan. We need love. We need to love God first. We need to love ourselves. We need to love others. It's just that simple. Once you start pouring out love from your life, more love is poured back into your life. That is not to say that you should go around doing good deeds because you want to benefit in some way because then, you have the wrong motives. But, just live in obedience to God each and every day. If you stumble, don't stay there; ask God for forgiveness and keep moving forward in love.

The bottom line is God is love. And, God is all we need. Everything else in life falls into place when He is at the center of it all. Choose to love and you choose to live the good life, even in the rough times. It is a love that will never fail.

Prayer

Thank You, God for Your example of the right way to love.
Please forgive me for not showing my love for You through obeying Your commands.
Lord, please help me to show love to the children of God and to love myself even when I feel unlovable.

In Jesus' Name,
Amen

Reflections for the Week

Read and meditate on this week's Scripture. Say the
prayer at the end of the devotion daily and ask for
God's wisdom. Write down any revelations or
reflections you may have throughout the week.

_____

_____

_____

_____

_____

_____

_____

_____

_____

_____

_____

_____

Week Thirty Three

Know Your Worth

Scripture:
Esther 1:12

But when the attendants delivered the king's command, Queen Vashti refused to come. Then the king became furious and burned with anger. (Read Esther Chapter 1)

Quote from *Pray While You're Prey*:

"I have met many [people who do not feel] worthy to truly have the best that God has to give..."

She walked into the gym, and the guys gawked and the women squawked. I looked up and thought, "Oh my, what was that poor child thinking when she left the house." She was dressed to the nines for a basketball game, and I guess there is nothing wrong with that; to each her own. What was wrong was that it was freezing cold, yet, her clothes were thin, and her midriff was exposed, along with all of her other assets. Upon closer inspection, it was clear that this young woman was, in fact, young. It broke my heart to see her flitting about, scantily clad, and flirting with anyone who would give her attention. I was nearly brought to tears to see this young sister sending out all of the wrong messages and not seeming to care what anyone thought of her.

There is nothing wrong with being an individual. In fact, being unique is wonderful. Still, each and every day, I see young women and young men who devalue themselves by how they speak, how they dress and how they act. But, we as the human race, and especially those of us who claim to be Christians, need to do better. Do we not understand that, when people see how you dress, act, talk, and walk, they make a decision about the God you serve based on how much you value yourself?

I love the story of Queen Vashti. Knowing that she had everything to lose for disobeying the king, she refused to make a spectacle of herself in front of him and his friends. Queen Vashti took a stand that too many of us, men and women, are unwilling to take. She knew that she was worthy of far more than being a showgirl for her husband. We, single Christians, and any Christian for that matter, must take and stand and know our worth.

When you are invited into a situation that will devalue you, run--don't walk--away! God will never bring someone into your life that is going to desire for you to act in a way that makes you look foolish. God does not give us mates that are willing to mortify us in front of their friends or family or co-workers. And, if you know your worth, you will not allow yourself to be put in such a predicament. Could it cost you your relationship? Yes! But, which relationship is more important, your relationship with someone who objectifies you, or, your relationship with the One who made you who you are.

The only way that we will ever receive the blessed mate that God wants to send us is if we know our worth. Too many single Christians think that they are unworthy of God's best and that kind of negative thinking can do unfathomable levels of harm. So, look yourself in the mirror, and remind yourself that you are fearfully and wonderfully made. And, never ever let anyone tell you otherwise.

Prayer

Thank You, God for helping me realize that I am worth of love and respect.
Please forgive me for allowing people in my life that do not respect me and for disrespecting myself.
Lord, please help me to hold my head up high and always stand for what is right.

In Jesus' Name,
Amen

Reflections for the Week

Read and meditate on this week's Scripture. Say the prayer at the end of the devotion daily and ask for God's wisdom. Write down any revelations or reflections you may have throughout the week.

_____

_____

_____

_____

_____

_____

_____

_____

_____

_____

_____

_____

Pray While You're Prey Weekly Devotions for Singles

Week Thirty Four

Purify

Scripture:
2 Corinthians 7:1

Therefore, since we have these promises, dear friends, let us purify ourselves from everything that contaminates body and spirit, perfecting holiness out of reverence for God.

Quote from *Pray While You're Prey*:

"Each and every human who confesses the Lord Jesus Christ as his or her Savior has a never-ending obligation to seek holiness and righteousness in every deed."

During the Lent season, forty days before Easter, many people of all different religions think of something to give up for forty days. I did not grow up observing Lent, so I do not know the purpose and I am sure that each person must search his or her heart to know their true purpose of observing Lent. From what I have observed, most people go on this fast in order to grow closer to God, which is always a good thing as far as I am concerned.

Some people choose to give up particular foods or drinks: fatty foods, fried foods, chocolate, carbonated drinks, or alcoholic drinks. Some people give up behaviors like watching television or hanging out with certain people. I can see how in choosing to sacrifice things that we love we can honor God and grow closer to Him as we deny our fleshly desires. But, why limit ourselves to just the Lent season.

Each and every day of our lives, we should be seeking to live a life that is a holy and acceptable sacrifice to God. We should constantly be seeking to purify ourselves. We should take inventory of our lives and notice any person or habit that has become an idol to us. We should be honest with ourselves and decide daily if we are putting God first in our lives or if we are living to please someone else, even if that someone else is the person we see in the mirror.

God sent Jesus to this earth to walk in human form and to show us that our lives can be lived without the filth and grime of sin. Yes, Jesus was God Son, but he was also human and faced with every temptation with which any of us could ever possibly be faced. And yet, Jesus was able to pass every test this world threw at Him, even unto death just so that He could show us how to live and to help us know that He is there for us.

Admittedly, there have been times when I thought about fasting from certain foods or behaviors and the thought of not getting my daily nap or not getting to eat a Snickers bar has been terrifying. However, there is nothing scarier than knowing that I am consciously making the choice to include filth in my life on a daily basis and I am justifying it by pointing out all of the "good things" that I do. No, napping, eating candy, or drinking soda is not the filth; allowing ungodly thoughts, words and actions into my life is the filth.

So, rather than trying to fast once a year, we all need to purify daily. We need to grow in Christ and grow closer to Christ. We must seek holiness and righteousness in every deed, and the only way to accomplish that successfully is through Christ who gives us strength.

Prayer

Thank You, God for giving us all an example of One who could live life free from all impurities. Please forgive me for ignoring areas of sin in my life. Lord, please help me to purify and die to self daily, so that I can live in holiness and reverence for you.

In Jesus' Name,
Amen

Reflections for the Week

Read and meditate on this week's Scripture. Say the prayer at the end of the devotion daily and ask for God's wisdom. Write down any revelations or reflections you may have throughout the week.

_____

_____

_____

_____

_____

_____

_____

_____

_____

_____

_____

_____

Pray While You're Prey Weekly Devotions for Singles

Week Thirty Five

When I Call You

Scripture:
Psalm 138:2

I will worship toward Your holy temple and praise
Your name for Your loving-kindness and for Your
truth and faithfulness; for You have exalted above all
else Your name and Your word and You have
magnified Your word above all Your name!

Quote from *Pray While You're Prey*:
"There have been many nights when I woke up with a
problem, or some sudden clarity, or just wanting to
talk. It was a wonderful feeling to know that I had a
friend who wouldn't curse me out for calling so late,
who would listen to every word I had to say, and who
would lead me down the best path that I could
choose."

Every day when I get off work, I call my mom for a
daily debrief. It gives me a chance to find out about
her day, give her a rundown of my day. I get a chance
to vent if something out of the ordinary happens and
my mom is a fantastic listener. It is a very rare
occasion that she interrupts me or offers unsolicited
advice. She talks and I listen. Then, I talk and she
listens. It is fantastic. But, there are some times when
I need someone to talk to and it is way too late to call
my mom or even one of my friends.

As fantastic as it is to talk to my mommy, it is awesome to know that I have a Heavenly Father that I can call on at any time. I really am not much of a talker anymore. I am a very introverted person and my mom is the main person with whom I talk for an extended period of time. I much prefer to write, e-mail, message, or text. And, the beautiful thing about God is that I never have to open my mouth to communicate with Him. All I have to do is open my heart.

While it is nice to have a family member or friend who we can always call, God desires to be the first Friend that we think of when we want to talk. He will always be available. If we have something great happen, He wants us to bring it to Him. When something hurts us, He wants us to bring it to Him. When we are excited, He wants us to share it with Him. When we are confused, He wants us to come to Him.

It's not that it is wrong to speak to someone else because God can use others to speak what He needs us to hear, but God wants us to seek His face first. In the Psalm, it says, "When I called, You answered me…." How many of your friends and family members can you say that about? Even though we may have the best intentions, it's impossible for us as human beings to be there for each other all of the time. So, thank God for God. Thank God for His omniscience and omnipresence. Thank

God that He can hear me call and you call and answer all of us at the same time. He's just good like that.

And, just like the psalmist, once we realize that when we call on the name of Jesus, something awesome is bound to happen, we can finally step boldly before the throne of grace and make our requests known to God. We can call on Him knowing that, whether it's early in the morning, late in the evening or in the middle of the day, He will listen, and He will answer. You are never alone. God hears you when you call Him.

Prayer

Thank You, God for answering me every single time I call on You.

Please forgive me for seeking help from anyone other than You.

Lord, please help me to remember that
You will always be there for me and have my best in mind.

In Jesus' Name,
Amen

Reflections for the Week

Read and meditate on this week's Scripture. Say the
prayer at the end of the devotion daily and ask for
God's wisdom. Write down any revelations or
reflections you may have throughout the week.

_____

_____

_____

_____

_____

_____

_____

_____

_____

_____

_____

_____

Week Thirty Six

Clean Inside

Scripture:
Matthew 23:26

First clean the inside of the cup and dish, and then
the outside also will be clean.

Quote from *Pray While You're Prey*:

"Jesus Christ was proof that we could be human and
not be filthy. Jesus Christ was proof that we could be
blameless and clean."

When I was younger and I wanted to play, but didn't
feel like thoroughly cleaning my room, I would just
make my bed, and then, shove things under the bed
and in the closet to make it look like I had done my
chores. Unfortunately for me, both of my parents
were Navy veterans, so I rarely got away with it.

Many of us try to dress up our outside while
completely ignoring our inside and we call it cleaning
up our lives. We make sure that we say the right
things, hang out with the right people, and get caught
doing the right activities. But, what is the use of
looking clean on the outside when you are dirty on
the inside?

Surely, we will all make mistakes because none of us
are perfect. Still, we need to make every effort to
clean up the messes in our lives. A season of

singleness is a fantastic time to do so. The single season is the perfect time to really focus on ourselves; not for the purpose of being selfish, but for the purpose of being more like Christ. We can go to our Father and ask Him to reveal to us the dirty places in our lives that we have hidden so well that we forgot they were there. I have to warn you, though, if you ask God for this, you must be prepared to be shocked.

Every time I think I am all cleaned up, I ask God to show my where I am falling short. And, when I do so, it is usually because I am fully confident that I have little to no dirty areas. But, oh my! God will place some people and some situations in your life to reveal the dirt that is still lingering well beneath the surface. I don't know about anyone else, but when God does bless me with a mate, I want to be the best person that I can be. Actually, if God never sends me a mate, I still want to be the best I can be for Him.

Has this ever happened to you? You're super thirsty, so you go to the cabinet and pull out a cup. You fill the cup with your favorite drink, take a couple of sips and then look in the cup and find some gunk the dishwasher left behind. The cup sure looked clean from the outside, but none of that matters if there is some nastiness on the inside. The same goes for us. We must all make sure that we are clean inside and God gave us a perfect example and a perfect sacrifice to be sure that we could be.

Prayer

Thank You, God for sending Your Son to be an
example of how to truly live a clean life.
Please forgive me for trying to cover up the dirt in
my life, as if you are not omniscient.
Lord, please help me to never be haughty enough
to think that there is not something inside of me that
can be cleaner.

In Jesus' Name,
Amen

Reflections for the Week

Read and meditate on this week's Scripture. Say the prayer at the end of the devotion daily and ask for God's wisdom. Write down any revelations or reflections you may have throughout the week.

_____

_____

_____

_____

_____

_____

_____

_____

_____

_____

_____

_____

Week Thirty Seven

When Fear Leads to Safety

Scripture:
Proverbs 14:26-27

Whoever fears the LORD has a secure fortress, and for their children it will be a refuge. The fear of the LORD is a fountain of life, turning a person from the snares of death.

Quote from *Pray While You're Prey*:

"I do not speak of fear in the sense of being scared, but in the sense of reverence and respect. Reverence and respect for God and God's Word lead to strong confidence, refuge, contentment, and salvation from death."

My dad has a booming voice. Small children are often afraid when he speaks in his "Mufasa" voice. For a lot of my life, it was that voice that kept me out of trouble. Not wanting to hear the disappointment in my father's voice or not wanting to hear the discipline in my father's voice was the cause for many decisions that I made in my life. I did not and do not fear my father, but he commands such authority that I do have an incredible level of respect for his opinion and his guidance.

Even though, when little children hear that big, booming voice, it scares the bejeezes out of them, they also know that the man behind that voice will protect them and care for them. There have been many occasions when I have seen my niece and nephews go from crying because my dad raised his voice to cuddling up in his lap of safety in a matter of seconds. It is because the voice may be scary, but the children innately know that behind that big voice is an even bigger heart that truly cares about their well-being.

It is the same with our relationship with God. If you read the Bible, and see how God dealt with disobedience, especially in the Old Testament, you might be fearful of Him. But, the proper response is to be obedient because of reverence for God. We should listen to His commands for our lives because we respect that He knows what is best. When we come to that place of reverence and respect, then God can keep us safe. When we surrender to His Will, we can lay at His feet and just worship without having a concern for any calamity or uncertainty that may surround our lives. This is the kind of fear that leads to safety.

If you ever watch scary movies, you will see that when people are being chased and are scared, they sometimes make irrational decisions that put them in more danger. For example, they run upstairs or into woods. This is not the type of fear that God desires for us to have of Him. He wants us to have a respectful fear of Him. He does not want us to be so scared that we jump into irrational decisions and unnatural situations. He wants us to allow Him to guide us into His safety. He wants us to experience our best lives the lives He has planned for us.

Prayer

Thank You, God for being a God whom I can love
and respect.
Please forgive me for allowing irrational fear to cloud
my judgment.
Lord, please help me to know that there is safety
in Your arms and that You will always lead me on the
best path.

In Jesus' Name,
Amen

Reflections for the Week

Read and meditate on this week's Scripture. Say the prayer at the end of the devotion daily and ask for God's wisdom. Write down any revelations or reflections you may have throughout the week.

_____

_____

_____

_____

_____

_____

_____

_____

_____

_____

_____

_____

Pray While You're Prey Weekly Devotions for Singles

Week Thirty Eight

No One Else

Scripture:
1Timothy 2:5

For there is one God and one mediator between God and mankind, the man Christ Jesus, who gave himself as a ransom for all people

Quote from *Pray While You're Prey*:

"I can only imagine how God feels when we act ashamed of Him or brush Him off, choosing things of this world over Him, because He definitely loves us and showed us the ultimate demonstration of love when he sacrificed His only Son."

Jesus was praised about a week before those same people praising Him would shout, "Crucify Him!" Jesus, the blameless, Almighty, all-powerful, Son of God would be heralded as a savior one week and pay the ultimate sacrifice the next week. And,

He chose to be that sacrifice despite the fact that the very people He came to save treated Him like garbage. But, let's not be so haughty as to condemn those people before we look in the mirror and ask ourselves how we treat Jesus.

This devotion series is not just about being content while you are single; it is about allowing yourself to be devoted to Christ. It is about finding comfort and solace in Him. Have you ever praised Jesus one week only to ignore Him the next? Perhaps, it did not even take a week. Maybe it was a few days or a few hours or, dare I say, just a few minutes. We, and I am including me, are quick to offer praise when Jesus is being who we think He should be. Yet, we are quick to question Him when the circumstances of our lives are not how we wish them to be. When we do that we are no different that the people who laid down palm branches to honor Him one day and spit on Jesus just a few days later.

Jesus could have said, "Daddy, I don't want to do this." Make no mistake about this, Jesus did not have to die for our sins. He showed a love that we cannot even fathom. He showed a love that NO ONE ELSE would dare show. Can you imagine dying for the people who treat you like dirt? I can't, but Jesus did. He gave Himself as a ransom for you and me and for all people; for anyone who would accept Him as Lord and Savior.

So, really examine your heart. Do you appreciate that no one else has done for you what Jesus did? No boyfriend, girlfriend, significant other or spouse could even come close to that kind of love. So, shouldn't we be more desperate to get close to the

One who died for us than we are for our human relationships. It is not that relationships are bad. I will be so grateful when God sends me my forever husband, but I cannot forget His sacrifice because no one else will ever love me that.

Prayer

Thank You, God for Your Son, Jesus Christ, the One
and Only mediator.
Please forgive me for taking Your Sacrifice
for granted and complaining or thinking that You
don't love me because I don't get my way.
Lord, please help me to always remember Your loving
gift at Calvary's cross and to Honor You above all
others.

In Jesus' Name,
Amen

Reflections for the Week

Read and meditate on this week's Scripture. Say the
prayer at the end of the devotion daily and ask for
God's wisdom. Write down any revelations or
reflections you may have throughout the week.

_____

_____

_____

_____

_____

_____

_____

_____

_____

_____

_____

_____

_____

Week Thirty Nine

Don't Hold Back

Scripture:
Deuteronomy 30:10

...Nothing halfhearted here; you must return to
GOD, your God, totally, heart and soul, holding
nothing back.

Quote from *Pray While You're Prey*:

"If we are among those chosen by God to have
eternal life, our goal should be to please God and to
be obedient. It is not easy, but it is also not
impossible."

When I was in high school, I had three friends with
whom I was very close. We were, in fact best friends,
from the beginning of freshman year. At some point
during my junior year, though, those friends decided
that they no longer wanted to be friends with me. In
the weeks after turning their backs on me, two of the
three friends, asked for forgiveness and we
reconciled. Though, we remain close throughout the
rest of high school, our relationships were never the
same, and shortly after high school, we lost touch.

The reason our relationship was not the same on my
end is because I never felt like I could totally be
myself or totally trust that I would not lose my friends

again. I would hold back certain opinions about their actions. I would dampen certain aspects of my personality because I did not want to feel the hurt I had felt again.

The way I was treated by my friends pales in comparison to the many ways I have betrayed God. Though I have known the Lord for a very long time, there were several periods in my life when I turned my back on Him. In those times, I justified my actions because I felt angry with God that I had not gotten my way, or I felt that my obedience was not rewarded, and therefore, was not worth it. I would throw bratty, hissy fits and just walk away from God. However, God never walked away from me. Each and every time I realized how foolish I was being, He welcomed me back into His arms. And, He didn't hold anything back.

Once I reconciled with God, He did not hold back His blessings and His favor. There were absolutely consequences for my disobedience because He did not hold back His chastisement and discipline either. You see, unlike us, God was not afraid to still be a good friend to me and to continue to give me all of Him. He was not afraid that I would leave again because He knew that my love for Him and His love for me would always bring me back. So, in return, it is my responsibility to show my love towards Him wholeheartedly, through obedience, holding nothing back.

We owe God our all; our everything should belong to Him, including our love, which is shown through obedience. We must love God totally and hold nothing back. We cannot allow the influences of this world to cause us to be halfhearted towards God. No one in the world has given you or me a sacrifice like

God has given us. It was a sacrifice that we did not even deserve. So, though, you may feel that you wish your life was in a different place right now, it is not an excuse to fail to give God your all. Don't hold back.

Prayer

Thank You, God for giving me boundaries
and for giving structure to my life, so that I know what I must do.
Please forgive me for being disobedient, for turning away from You
and for the times when I am not fully and totally committed to Your will.
Lord, please help me to keep Your commandments and to walk on the path that you have set out for me.

In Jesus' Name,
Amen

Reflections for the Week

Read and meditate on this week's Scripture. Say the prayer at the end of the devotion daily and ask for God's wisdom. Write down any revelations or reflections you may have throughout the week.

_____

_____

_____

_____

_____

_____

_____

_____

_____

_____

_____

_____

Pray While You're Prey Weekly Devotions for Singles

Week Forty

Still Blessed

Scripture:
1 Peter 3:13-14

Who is going to harm you if you are eager to do good?
But even if you should suffer for what is right, you are
blessed.

Quote from *Pray While You're Prey*:

"I cannot stress enough that if you follow God's will,
He will bless you."

Have you gotten them? I have. The looks that scream,
"I wonder what is wrong with her," or, "She must
have some major issue." Or, have you gotten the
whispers behind your back that are trying to figure
out why you are still single, or, why you are single
with no children? Worse yet, has someone come up
to your face and told you why you are still single, or,
that at the rate you are going, you will never have
children of your own.

It's amazing to me what people think is their business.
And, often, they truly believe they are doing you a
favor. They feel like you are not painfully aware of
your singleness, so they should help you figure out
your situation. The proverbial "they" says things like,

"Stop being so uptight and picky, girl," or, "Don't you think it's time for you to settle down, man." "They" say these things when, ultimately, the timing and length of your single season as a Christian is between you and the God who made you. No one else gets a say.

What "they" fail to realize, other than it is none of their cotton-picking business, is that maybe, just maybe, you are being obedient. I cannot speak for everyone who is single; however, for those of us who are trying to live in God's will for our lives, we should be eager to do this single thing God's way. God promises us so many times and in so many ways that if we are obedient to Him, we are still blessed.

Imagine that you compromise and settle for someone who does not match the one for whom you have prayed to God. Exactly how blessed, joyful, and peaceful do you feel that relationship will be? How long do you think it will last? Sure, it might temporarily ease the pain and suffering of loneliness, but at what cost? If a man settles down to soon, before he is ready to love his wife as Christ loved the church, how will that relationship fare? I can tell you from experience that it does not end well in many cases.

So, no matter what anyone in this world says, if you are living in your single season in a way that is pleasing to God, no one can harm you. Do not let the pressures of this world make you feel like there is something wrong with you because you do not have a mate or children. God makes everything beautiful in His timing. One day, the times of suffering will be a distant memory. In the meantime, if someone has the nerve to point out that you are "still single," kindly remind that person that you are also, "still blessed!"

Prayer

Thank You, God for the comfort in knowing that
there is a blessing in obedience.
Please forgive me for allowing others to
infiltrate my beliefs
about where You have me in this season of my
life.
Lord, please help me to appreciate all of the
blessings
and mercies that you give me daily as I follow Your
will.

In Jesus' Name,
Amen

Reflections for the Week

Read and meditate on this week's Scripture. Say the
prayer at the end of the devotion daily and ask for
God's wisdom. Write down any revelations or
reflections you may have throughout the week.

_____

_____

_____

_____

_____

_____

_____

_____

_____

_____

_____

_____

_____

Pray While You're Prey Weekly Devotions for Singles

Week Forty One

Who Can Quench My Thirst For Love?

Scripture:
Song of Solomon 8:7

Many waters cannot quench love; rivers cannot sweep
it away...

Quote from *Pray While You're Prey*:

"Some of the most beautiful love poetry and stories
can be found right in the Bible. If you're looking for a
good romance novel, thumb through Song of
Solomon sometime.... I mean, I wouldn't mind
having a man after me who thought that "many
waters cannot quench love; neither can the floods
drown it.""

Have you ever read Song of Solomon? Some of it is a
bit racy and, admittedly, could make you
uncomfortable. Nevertheless, the book has some of
the most beautiful representations of love and
courtship that have ever been written in any literary
work.

In Chapter 8, verse 7, it says, "Many waters cannot
quench love; rivers cannot sweep it away." That is
some deep love!

You know when you are thirsty, I mean dehydrated, it seems like nothing will satisfy your thirst. You may drink a soda, and it is sweet, but you are still thirsting for something else. You may drink milk, and it can usually take away a bad taste in your mouth or soothe a burning mouth, but you still are not satisfied. You can drink juice and you usually feel good about its nutrients, but it does not fill you. You can drink tea or coffee and they make you feel all warm and fuzzy and give you energy, but the thirst is not quenched. When you are really thirsty, the only thing that will satisfy that thirst is pure, unadulterated water.

For a lot of my life, I was thirsty for love. For as long as I can remember, I just wanted to have a boyfriend to date or a husband to marry. My whole existence became my search for the perfect mate. I have dated sweet guys who have made me feel beautiful and smart. They told me everything I longed to hear, so that they could get what they wanted from me. And, after my experiences with them, I felt empty. None of my relationships could quench my thirst for love. I found out why.

The innate desire that we have to love and be loved comes from being formed in the image of God and Christ. God is Love.

Jesus Christ is Love. No man or woman can satisfy a Christian's need for love. Only the Living Water will end the thirsting in your soul. You can drink a whole entire river or potential mates, have floods and floods of dates, but until you fall wholly and completely in love with the true and living God, no other love (or like or lust) will be satisfying. It is in Him alone that we find the sole satisfaction for our souls.

Once, we know that love and fully experience that level of love, we will not feel thirsty whether in a relationship or single. Any relationship that comes our way will be an added bonus, but, even if we do not have a relationship with a significant other, we can still feel full and whole.

Prayer

Thank You, God for loving me with a love with which no other can compare.
Please forgive me for longing for something or someone else to satisfy a thirst that is only quenched by You.
Lord, please help me to know that I am whole with Your love and Your love alone.

In Jesus' Name,
Amen

Reflections for the Week

Read and meditate on this week's Scripture. Say the
prayer at the end of the devotion daily and ask for
God's wisdom. Write down any revelations or
reflections you may have throughout the week.

_____

_____

_____

_____

_____

_____

_____

_____

_____

_____

_____

_____

Pray While You're Prey Weekly Devotions for Singles

Week Forty Two

It's Not You, It's Me

Scripture:
1 Samuel 8:7

And the LORD told him: "Listen to all that the people are saying to you; it is not you they have rejected, but they have rejected Me...

Quote from *Pray While You're Prey*:

"I'm leaning and depending on God to send me someone who truly appreciates me and knows how to treat me."

I personally have not been the subject of many sorry excuses for a break up. In my whole, three, real, serious relationships, I have always been the one to call it quits officially. And, in my not-so- real relationships, I never really got a reason; generally, the guy just stopped calling or returning calls. I have heard, however, that a line that is often used in ending relationships is,

"It's not you, it's me."

This line is usually given with the party doing the breaking up does not want to hurt the feelings of the party with whom he or she is breaking up. So, rather than explain why the relationship did not work, the person begins to list all of his or her faults, flaws, or emotional baggage.

Well, it is my understanding that this particular method of ending a relationship, though popular, may not have the intended effects. For example, the jilted party may feel ignorant for not noticing how messed up his or her partner had been. Or, the party being left may feel that he or she should get the opportunity to "fix" the other person. In the end, someone's feelings will be hurt anyway, so honesty is the best policy.

While the "it's not you, it's me" break up may not be as useful as people think, the concept may help many single Christians understand why they are still in a state of singleness. Do you have people telling you that you are too picky? Has someone broken up with you or not even asked you out because you are too uptight or conservative? If you are living the life that God has asked you to live, the people who don't want to date or marry you are not rejecting you; they are rejecting the God in you.

Some people simply cannot handle the life that you live by faith. And, I am not saying to get all high and mighty and stick your good Christian nose in the air, but I am saying that some people cannot handle the masterpiece that God made you to be. So, let's really examine this: Do you really want to spend the rest of your life or even one more minute with someone who is threatened by your relationship with Christ? I, for sure, do not.

So, the next time someone rejects you or breaks up with you, hear God's voice saying, "It is not you they have rejected, but they have rejected Me." If you desire to be in a relationship, it should be with someone who loves and appreciates you for all that you are through Christ. And, as such, that person should treat you like the precious commodity that you are to your Father. If he or she cannot accept the God in you, then it is best for that person to keep it moving, so the one that God has for you can enter into your life.

Prayer
Thank You, God for Your grace and Your mercies that help me to live a life that is pleasing to You and only You.
Please forgive me for getting caught up in the rejection of those who are in love with this word.
Lord, please help me to hold out for someone who is willing to seek You to find me.

In Jesus' Name,
Amen

Reflections for the Week

Read and meditate on this week's Scripture. Say the
prayer at the end of the devotion daily and ask for
God's wisdom. Write down any revelations or
reflections you may have throughout the week.

_____

_____

_____

_____

_____

_____

_____

_____

_____

_____

_____

_____

_____

Pray While You're Prey Weekly Devotions for Singles

Week Forty Three

Sheer Delight

Scripture:
Psalm 37:4-5

Take delight in the LORD, and He will give you the desires of your heart. Commit your way to the LORD;
trust also in Him; and He shall bring it to pass.

Quote from *Pray While You're Prey*:

"I know the type of [mate] that I desire, and I want to be with the type of [mate] that God desires for me."

I, like many, have often searched for the key to getting everything I want. I mean, who doesn't like getting his or her way? I will even admit, because I know I have been forgiven for it, that there was a point in which I thought I could manipulate God.

I would say things like, "God, I promise to…If You will…," (you didn't really think I was going to fill in the blanks, did you?). Then, I read this Scripture, Psalm 37:4, "Delight yourself in the Lord and He will give you the desires of your heart." It sounded super simple.

So, I just had to show God that I loved Him, right? I went to church, Sunday school, and Bible Study. I paid my tithes and offering. I sang with the praise team. I even read the Bible and prayed on my own. And, I am a deacon's daughter, so that had to count for something. And, I truly felt that because I did all of that, God should give me what I wanted...A MAN!!!

I would pray this Scripture back to Him like I was told you are supposed to, "Lord, You said if I delight in You, You would give me the desires of my heart, so I want a man. Remember, what You promised. I am delighting in You." Yes, I was that brazen, or young and stupid either way, I was totally misinterpreting this verse and I had taken it out of context.

I never really read the second part of the verse about commitment and trust. Not only that, but I did not realize that when you are serving someone only for what you can get out of the deal, that is not true devotion. I have learned through many of my relationships with men, friends and family, how I was treating God. I have had many people in my life offer me praise, help, and so-called commitment, just so that they could get what they wanted from me. It is an awful feeling and I hate that I ever thought that my relationship with God should be like that. But, praise God for spiritual growth!!!

Now, I know that these verses mean when you have sheer delight in God alone, you commit to Him alone, and you trust in Him alone, He will change your heart and your desires to conform to His Will for your life. He will set you on a path of dreams that you never even imagined. All of the things and people you wanted before may be included, but they will not be the ultimate prize. The ultimate prize will be an intimate relationship with the only One who can totally and completely satiate your every desire, which is the one, true, living, loving God Almighty. Find sheer delight and Him and see your desires fulfilled.

Prayer

Thank You, God for allowing me to have a close, personal relationship with You.
Please forgive me for anytime I have done something to please You in an effort to get my way.
Lord, please help me to wholly commit to Your Will for my life
and trust in You, so that the dreams You placed me will come to pass.

In Jesus' Name,
Amen

Reflections for the Week

Read and meditate on this week's Scripture. Say the prayer at the end of the devotion daily and ask for God's wisdom. Write down any revelations or reflections you may have throughout the week.

_____

_____

_____

_____

_____

_____

_____

_____

_____

_____

_____

_____

Pray While You're Prey Weekly Devotions for Singles

Week Forty Four

Guess Who's Coming to Dinner

Scripture:
Revelation 3:20

Here I am! I stand at the door and knock. If anyone
hears My voice and opens the door, I will come in
and eat with that person, and they with Me.

Quote from *Pray While You're Prey*:

"There are so many people in the world who have yet
to discover the wonders of God. While we sit and
complain about the things that we don't have, do we
ever stop to think about how fortunate we are to have
Christ?"

I love to eat! I especially like to go to a nice restaurant
and enjoy a delectable meal. As a singleton, that
usually means that I am dining alone. There was a
time when I would not eat at restaurants because I
was afraid that people would stare at me or pity me
because I was dining alone. So, when a new restaurant
opened, I would envy every person who got to go and
enjoy the restaurant with their significant other. I
would whine and complain about how unfair it was
that I would never get to go to these nice places to
enjoy a meal because I had no one with whom to
dine.

Then, on one vacation, I decided that, rather than order takeout, visit a drive-thru, or get room service, I would go to different restaurants. I would go and enjoy dinner all by myself. After all, I was on vacation by myself and I was in a town where no one knew me, so they could not judge me for eating alone. Eventually, I got the hang of dining alone. I no longer denied myself the experience of trying new restaurants just because I had no one special in my life with whom to dine.

There are many times when we get so caught up in what we do not have that we start to drown in our loneliness. It is as if, because we are single, everything else about our lives has to be miserable. However, if you find yourself having that kind of defeated mindset, you are well- served to not enter into a relationship anytime soon. In a relationship, there should be two people who feel victorious and whole on their own that come together to create something powerful.

If you will listen, you will hear that God is knocking at the door of your heart. He wants your attention. He wants your adoration. God wants to spend time with you. God, the very same God who created heaven and earth and everything in it that you desire, cares enough for you that He wants some alone time with you. He knocks, but will you answer? Or, will you be so busy weeping and wailing and crying, "Woe is me!" that you don't even notice that the Savior is waiting to enter your heart. He wants to make you feel whole and complete in Him. So that, mate or no mate, you are never alone. Listen to His voice and let Him into your heart fully. Dine with Him daily. Feast on His Word. Drink from His well of Living Water.

Prayer

Thank You, God for giving me the opportunity to
dine with You and commune with You.
Please forgive me for thinking that there is something
missing from my life.
Lord, please help me to hear You and accept Your
will for my life.

In Jesus' Name,
Amen

Reflections for the Week

Read and meditate on this week's Scripture. Say the
prayer at the end of the devotion daily and ask for
God's wisdom. Write down any revelations or
reflections you may have throughout the week.

_____

_____

_____

_____

_____

_____

_____

_____

_____

_____

_____

_____

Pray While You're Prey Weekly Devotions for Singles

Week Forty Five

A New Understanding

Scripture:
Romans 12:3 *The Message*

The only accurate way to understand ourselves is by
what God is and by what He does for us, not by what
we are and what we do for Him."

Quote from *Pray While You're Prey*:

"Do you believe that God is sovereign and that He
has a plan for your life?"

There are times when I find myself trying to figure
God out. I find myself trying to make sense of what is
happening in my life and trying to guess God's next
move. It is all really very silly. God has ways and
thoughts that are so much higher than anything that
we could ever conceive (Isaiah 55).

I think to myself that if I do the right things and say
the right things, then there should be certain
outcomes. However, my focus is all wrong. In order
to understand my life and to understand my purpose,
I cannot look at what I do or say or think. I have to
look at who God is and what He does for me.

In the context of singleness, I have spent many years trying to figure out the right clothes to wear, the right words to say, the proper ways to flirt, so as to not upset the Father. I have tried to stay away from certain places, so I do not embarrass the Father. I have tried to sing, praise and give to impress the Father. Sometimes, I do all of this, in an effort to get a mate, not to discover who God is and what He means to me.

In doing so, I tell God that He is not enough for me. When I start to believe that I am who I am because of what I do, I am leaving God out of the equation. And, I know that I am not the only person who knows for a fact that there would be no me without Him. In the season of singleness, there is an opportunity for self-discovery. There is a chance to understand who we are, not as a spouse or parent, not defined by our career or ministry, but defined by what God is and what He does for us.

Use this time to discover, to understand to unravel, the beauty created in you by God's grace, His mercy, His love and His favor. Allow that to satisfy your soul. Lonely times will come, but if you understand who you are in Christ, you can make it to the other side. Know that God is sovereign, and He has a plan for you that is not defined by what you do for Him, but what He does for you!

Prayer

Thank You, God for being sovereign and for having a
plan for my life.
Please forgive me for trying to understand myself
outside of who You are and what You have done for
me.
Lord, please help me to trust that You
always know what is best and that my purpose is
found in You.

In Jesus' Name,
Amen

Reflections for the Week

Read and meditate on this week's Scripture. Say the
prayer at the end of the devotion daily and ask for
God's wisdom. Write down any revelations or
reflections you may have throughout the week.

_____

_____

_____

_____

_____

_____

_____

_____

_____

_____

_____

Week Forty Six

Don't Forget to Pray

Scripture:
James 1:5-8 *The Message*

If you don't know what you're doing, pray to the
Father. He loves to help. You'll get His help and
won't be condescended to when you ask for it. Ask
boldly, believingly, without a second thought. People
who "worry their prayers" are like wind-whipped
waves. Don't think you're going to get anything from
the Master that way, adrift at sea, keeping all your
options open.

Quote from *Pray While You're Prey*:

"I hope to learn and to teach others to PRAY..."

The title of my book and this devotion series is, *Pray
While You're Prey*. While it may seem like much of the
focus is on the second "prey," the issue of singleness,
most of the focus should be on the first "pray." It
never ceases to amaze me that God wants to
communicate with me. Who am I that He is
concerned about me? Who am I that He should even
care? God created heaven and earth and everything in
it. He hung the sun, the moon, and the stars. He gave
life to plants, animals, man and woman. He is all-
knowing, ever-present and all powerful. Why would
He, as great as He is, wants to talk to a speck of dust
like me?

Simply, He wants to talk to me because I am His. God doesn't want us to worship Him out of religion and routine. God wants a relationship. He wants us to worship Him in spirit and in truth. How can we be our true selves before God if we do not communicate with Him? God desires intimacy, authenticity, and dependency. He wants to help. But, we have to stop thinking that our issues are too small to bother God. We have to stop thinking that God is a genie meant to grant wishes. We need to start thinking about how we like those we love to communicate with us.

Imagine a relationship in which the person you love only talks to you when he or she needs something. Imagine a relationship in which your significant other does not want to share the intimate details of his or her feelings. The difference is that in human relationships, we may never know what is hidden deep within, but God always knows our innermost thoughts and desires. He is just wondering why we don't bring them to Him.

Imagine a relationship where one person does all the talking and never listens. Communication is two ways. Yes, God wants to hear our thoughts, our pains, our joys, our desires, our victories, but He also wants us to listen. He wants us to come to Him boldly and believing that He and He alone has the answer. We need to not go to God worried that He won't answer. While we might not always hear the answer we want to hear, we have to know that God's answer is best and that there is no other option, but to follow His path.

If you find yourself feeling empty, exasperated, exhausted, truly ask yourself if you have been communicating with God. Trust me, I know it is easy to run to a friend or family member with every thought or concern, but as well-meaning as that person may be, we cannot forget to pray. We must keep the lines of communication open with the Loving Father who only wants our best for his glory!

Prayer

Thank You, God for being a God that I don't have to be scared to talk to.
Please forgive me for running to others when I need to cast my cares upon You.
Lord, please help me to never be lax in my communication and relationship with You.

In Jesus' Name,
Amen

Reflections for the Week

Read and meditate on this week's Scripture. Say the
prayer at the end of the devotion daily and ask for
God's wisdom. Write down any revelations or
reflections you may have throughout the week.

_____

_____

_____

_____

_____

_____

_____

_____

_____

_____

_____

_____

_____

Pray While You're Prey Weekly Devotions for Singles

Week Forty Seven

Patiently Waiting

Scripture:
2 Chronicles 19:11

Act with courage, and may the LORD be with those
who do well.

Quote from *Pray While You're Prey*:

"My problem with asking [God] for what I want is
not being able to wait for Him to give it to me."

One day, I went to get a pedicure. I arrived and was
greeted cheerfully by the owner. She and her
employee were busy with clients, but she told me to
have a seat in the chair and one of them would be
with me or another employee would arrive. I settled
into the chair, a massage chair, and just relaxed and
waited. It was about forty-five minutes before the
employee arrived that was supposed to do my
pedicure. There were more apologies, and then, I got
one of the best, most-relaxing, beautifully-done
pedicures that I have ever gotten. I even got to
continue sitting in the massage chair while my toes
dried. After a while, it was hard to get up, but I had to
eat dinner. In that moment, I realized that waiting
patiently is not all that bad. The experience ended up
being rewarding, and did I mention, relaxing.

As I sat to write this devotion, I realize that I only used the word "patience" once in the book, *Pray While You're Prey*, I never knew that. In retrospect, I would imagine that it is because patience has been an issue for me. Waiting on God has been an issue for me. When I want something, I want it when I want it and how I want it. But God has shown me that it is best for me to wait for what He wants for me, when He wants it and how He wants it because what He wants for me surpasses every expectation of which I could ever dream.

It is not easy to wait patiently. It takes faith and courage. Right now, I have students who, with good intentions, are trying to think of people for me to date. They are teenagers and thirty-five seems really old to them, so they cannot wrap their brains around the fact that I am not married and do not have any children. To be honest, it is hard for me to wrap my brain around it at times. I look at my friends who have husbands and are having babies or even watching children graduate from high school and I wonder if it will ever be my turn. Yet I know that God has an amazing plan for my life, so I have to wait on Him, not just in my singleness, but for my career moves and for everything in my life.

Others may not understand why I or you do not just step out and make something happen. That is okay. Trust me, I have tried things my way and I like God's way much better. It is not always the easy way or the fastest way, but it is the way that is worth it! Because He is THE WAY, THE TRUTH, and THE LIFE. Wait patiently on God. Don't stop living your life; just surrender your life to God and allow Him to move. Waiting patiently is an act of courage and He will be with you.

Prayer

Thank You, God for being a God that may delay, but
does not deny my desires.
Please forgive me for trying to rush You into giving
me what I want.
Lord, please help me to wait with expectation that I
will receive Your favor for Your glory

In Jesus' Name,
Amen

Reflections for the Week

Read and meditate on this week's Scripture. Say the
prayer at the end of the devotion daily and ask for
God's wisdom. Write down any revelations or
reflections you may have throughout the week.

_____

_____

_____

_____

_____

_____

_____

_____

_____

_____

_____

_____

Pray While You're Prey Weekly Devotions for Singles

Week Forty Eight

Do Not Settle

Scripture:
1 John 3:21-22

Dear friends, if our hearts do not condemn us, we have confidence before God and receive from him anything we ask, because we keep his commands and do what pleases Him.

Quote from *Pray While You're Prey*:

"…women have been so indoctrinated with the ideas that we need to get married and that a single

woman is a second-class citizen that we may not realize that being a married woman is way too high on our priority list. As a result, we may make compromises during our hunt that we wouldn't normally make, all for the sake of not being alone."

A while back, I received a call from the car dealership where I leased my vehicle. They said that they wanted my car back early. They said that they needed used cars like mine that were well taken care of and would make sure that I drove off in a newer car at an affordable price. I went into the dealership; I met a salesman who seemed nice enough. I explained why I was there, that I did not have much time, and that I just wanted to explore my options. Well, they took my keys to "check out my car," took me on a test drive, and then started this very long process of trying to harass me into settling for a new car with a huge increase in payment. I stood up, demanded to have my car keys, and left.

Weeks later, I got a call from the same dealership, with the same speech. I told the person on the phone that it was my intention to NEVER visit that dealership again because they treated me as if I was an idiot and held me hostage. The salesman begged me to give them another chance. So, I did. I went in, I confidently told the salesman what price range would make me leave with a new car; not one penny over it. I let him know that I was not in the mood for any games. Though the paperwork process seemed to take a really long time, my old car was taken back by the dealership and I drove off in a new car with the payment that I asked for and a care package at no extra cost.

If I had compromised a few months ago, I would have regretted it. There was a part of me that wanted to settle just so that I did not have to deal with the decision of what to do with my car. Nevertheless, I stuck to my guns, and this time around, I demanded respect and integrity. I got what I desired and then some.

For the sake of not feeling alone or not feeling like a failure, how many times do we settle? How many times do we forget that our God is greater than our circumstances and if we will wait on Him, He will fulfill our every need? How many times do we ask Him to bless us, but then ignore His commands or live a life that is not pleasing to Him? This is not a story about God blessing me with a car because I am some perfect Christian. Yes, He gets all honor and praise for my new car. Still, I know that nothing I did or ever will do merits His favor and saving grace. Yet, God is willing to allow us to not have to compromise for less than we deserve when we are confident in Him and live according to His Word. So, trust God only and do not settle.

Prayer

Thank You, God for being a God that hears my prayers and answers them with the best answer at the right time.
Please forgive me for not believing that You will keep Your promises and settling for things of this world. Lord, please help me to hold out until my change comes.

In Jesus' Name,
Amen

Reflections for the Week

Read and meditate on this week's Scripture. Say the
prayer at the end of the devotion daily and ask for
God's wisdom. Write down any revelations or
reflections you may have throughout the week.

_____

_____

_____

_____

_____

_____

_____

_____

_____

_____

_____

_____

_____

Pray While You're Prey Weekly Devotions for Singles

Week Forty Nine

Hold On

Scripture:
Psalm 18:30

As for God, His way is perfect: The LORD's Word is flawless; He shields all who take refuge in Him.

Quote from *Pray While You're Prey*:

"…knowing what I know now, I will make sure that I move closer and closer to God to avoid past mistakes."

I know a lot of people who say that the Bible is outdated. They think that the Bible was written so long ago that it should be changed to apply to the way we live today. For me, I have come to realize that the Bible is God's perfect, living Word. I know this because, at different points in my life, God gives me something completely new in each passage of Scripture. It is not that the Bible that is some antiquated instrument of oppression that needs to be rewritten, it is that our hearts need to be transformed. We need to cling to God and not to this world.

I will admit that it is easier said than done. Following God's Word is not simple, but it is right. Does accepting God's salvation and following His Word mean that life becomes sunshine and rainbows every day? No, but it tells us this in God's Word. Following God's way leads to the loss of those things in our lives that are detrimental and unnecessary, but that does not make it hurt less when we lose relationships or go through suffering. However, when I start to think about whining about squeezing through the narrow gate, I think about how much more suffering Christ went through just to save my life; a worthless life that He did not need to save. Yet, His compassion was so great that He lived in a perfect way, suffered torture and died, so that I could live forever.

So, what do we need to do? We need to trust God. We need to believe His Word and His promises. We need to hold on! Yes, if you look around at the world and the people in it, it will seem like God is holding out on you. The devil has been using that lie since Adam and Eve. It seems like it is more beneficial to live the world's way. It seems that you will have more success in life, career, and relationships if you just follow the world. It seems this way, but that is deceptive.

God's way is perfect. If we just move close to Him, and take refuge in Him, He will shield us. There will be rough times. We are human beings and we have emotions. There will be times when you feel lonely or like a failure. There will be times when it doesn't seem like living God's Way is worth it, but those are the times when you have to press in to Him. Continue to follow

His perfect Way, continue to read His flawless Word, and continue to seek His will for your life. If you are saved, this is just the beginning of your life. There is a whole, new world after this one. You have eternity to think about and not just what this temporal life has to offer. I believe that holding on will be worth it.

Prayer

Thank You, God for being perfect in ALL of Your
Ways.
Please forgive me for trying to accomplish things in
my own way.
Lord, please help me to take refuge
in Your loving arms, so You can shield me.

In Jesus' Name,

Amen

Reflections for the Week

Read and meditate on this week's Scripture. Say the
prayer at the end of the devotion daily and ask for
God's wisdom. Write down any revelations or
reflections you may have throughout the week.

_____

_____

_____

_____

_____

_____

_____

_____

_____

_____

_____

_____

Pray While You're Prey Weekly Devotions for Singles

Week Fifty

What is Love?

Scripture:
1 John 4:7-8

Dear friends, let us love one another, for love comes from God. Everyone who loves has been born of God and knows God. Whoever does not love does not know God, because God is love.

Quote from *Pray While You're Prey*:

"I realize that I have to know and love all that is good about me in order to attract people who are good for me."

It is an age-old question…what is love? What does love mean? What does it mean to love someone? What does is meant to be in love? Often times, love is equated with a person with whom one shares an intimate relationship. But, the true meaning of love is not found in the dictionary or by some life quest for it; the meaning is found in the instruction manual for life: the Bible.

Perhaps, we ask the wrong questions. Maybe we should not ask, "What is love?" but rather, "Who is Love?" You see, the

Bible explains that God is love. It is that simple, yet we make it so complex. Because we know that God is love, we need to look no further than His character to know all about love. Love is a verb, not a noun; it requires action. Love is sacrifice. Love is putting others' needs before yours. Love is forgiveness. Love is kindness. Love is patience and endurance. And, how do I know that this is love? Because God is love and He does all of these things towards me and all of His children.

In many of the secular songs about love, love is either equated to sex or being hurt. That is not God's love. That is the world's love. The adage "You always hurt the ones you love" should not ring true for the Christian. This should not be the standard because the Bible clearly says that if you do not love you do not know God.

On the contrary, the famous line, "Love means never having to say you're sorry…" is also a misnomer. We are human and we will make mistakes. In order to be forgiven, we must recognize when we have treated someone badly. Sometimes, the person we need to apologize to the most to, after God, is ourselves. How can you know love and be loved if you cannot love yourself? This is not about being conceited, narcissistic, selfish or self- involved; it is about loving yourself enough to treat your whole self well. It is about embracing the awesome gifts that God has given you for the uplifting of His Kingdom.

At times, we focus so much on being figuring out what love is and how to attain it that we forget the simple truth that God is love. If we live following His example, loving others, and loving ourselves, we will have a level of contentment that will allow us to accept whatever God has for our lives. Does that mean you will never get lonely? Absolutely not; nonetheless, when those times come, the Supplier of ALL of your needs is still there for you, loving you and embracing you, if you let Him. He is love, and, in His appointed time, if it is His will, you will love and be loved by someone who is worthy of who God has made you to be.

Prayer

Thank You, God for being the very existence of Love and for giving us so many examples of true love. Please forgive me for not loving myself or others

the way that you have taught us to love.
Lord, please help me to show and to be love so that others may see You in me.

In Jesus' Name,
Amen

Reflections for the Week

Read and meditate on this week's Scripture. Say the prayer at the end of the devotion daily and ask for God's wisdom. Write down any revelations or reflections you may have throughout the week.

_____

_____

_____

_____

_____

_____

_____

_____

_____

_____

_____

_____

Pray While You're Prey Weekly Devotions for Singles

Week Fifty One

Plugged In, Not Charging

Scripture:
Deuteronomy 10:12-13

So now Israel, what do you think GOD expects from you? Just this: Live in his presence in holy reverence, follow the road he sets out for you, love him, serve GOD, your God, with everything you have in you, obey the commandments and regulations of GOD that I'm commanding you today—live a good life.

Quote from *Pray While You're Prey*:

"With or without a mate, I can live a full life that is pleasing to God, and I will be rewarded."

I turned on my laptop the other day and I noticed that, even though it had been plugged in all night, the battery was nearly dead. I restarted the computer and got a message that my charger was not compatible with the battery. However, I was still able to use the laptop because the AC adapter was working; it just wasn't charging the battery. So, I googled what the computer said was the issue, "plugged in, not charging."

This has been going on for a few days, but on this day, it hit me that this is exactly how I feel sometimes with my relationship with Christ. I feel like I am plugged in and not charging. In other words, I know that Christ and I are connected, but I feel stagnant in my life. I feel like I am not moving forward with Him. I feel drained.

Yes, I go to church. I worship sincerely. I read my Bible daily. I read devotions. I pray. I try to live a life that is pleasing to God. I am not trying to sound like the Pharisee that was praying in the New Testament. I am just wondering if there is anyone else that has felt plugged in, yet still empty. You feel like you are doing everything that you know to do. You are seeking God to find out what else you need to do. Why are you stuck in this place? Why can't you move into the next phase of your life?

Well, as I continued to troubleshoot the laptop/battery/charger issue, I noticed a common theme with this problem. The issue generally happened when using a universal charger. That is what I have because it was less expensive than ordering a new part from the company where I bought my computer. And, as I read through several pages that said, "Don't use a universal charger," I had an epiphany. Maybe I feel like I am plugged in, but not charging because I am using a universal standard with which to measure my life rather that the standard of the original Source of my life.

So many times, we get caught up in what the world says our lives should be. And, although we pray and praise, we feel like something is being held back from us. We are plugged in with universal chargers and we are not charging. Instead, we must rely on God; live in His presence, with holy reverence. We must realize that there is no universal formula for each of our lives. Rather, God has a unique and individual plan for each and every one of us to live a good life; a full life. And, what is more, for those who believe in Him and accept His Son, Jesus Christ, as Lord and Savior, that life never ends. It will continue throughout eternity. We must trust in His plan for our lives, so that we do not find ourselves plugged in, but not charging.

Prayer
Thank You, God for providing me with
every opportunity to have a full life on Earth and in
Heaven.
Please forgive me for thinking that You are holding
anything back from me.
Lord, please help me to not just be plugged in to
You, but recharged daily by Your Word, Your
guidance and Your grace.

In Jesus' Name,
Amen

Reflections for the Week

Read and meditate on this week's Scripture. Say the
prayer at the end of the devotion daily and ask for
God's wisdom. Write down any revelations or
reflections you may have throughout the week.

_____

_____

_____

_____

_____

_____

_____

_____

_____

_____

_____

_____

Pray While You're Prey Weekly Devotions for Singles

Week Fifty Two

The End Result

Scripture:
1 Thessalonians 3:12-13

May the Lord make your love increase and overflow
for each other and for everyone else, just as ours does
for you. May he strengthen your hearts so that you
will be blameless and holy in the presence of our God
and Father when our Lord Jesus comes with all his
holy ones.

Quote from *Pray While You're Prey*:

"We are not called to be holy to unlock a toy store
full of blessings; we are called to holiness to share
God's goodness with others and to spread the Gospel
of Christ."

What is the point of knowing love and showing love
without a true and intimate relationship with God
through Jesus Christ? When I first published *Pray
While You're Prey*, I sent a copy to a friend of mine.
She wrote me back that she thought the book was
good even for non-Christians. The conversation was
one I will never forget because that was the day that I
found out that a young woman who had been like a
sister to me had "fallen in love" with someone who
convinced her that Jesus was not who the Bible says

He is. She no longer believed in the very Person that had caused us to have an almost decade-long bond. I was crushed and devastated because that was the beginning of the loss of that friendship, but not only that, I could not understand how anyone who claims to love a person could lead them away from the love of God.

I did not write a book to tell people how to date and have good relationships. The book and this devotion series are not some sort of how -to manual for finding a mate. If anyone believes that, he or she has completely missed the point. These are testimonies of how God has shown me, in times of obedience and disobedience, that He is God. This is about how no love surpasses His love because He is love. This is about dealing with our human emotions in a Godly manner that results in the uplifting of the Kingdom.

I hope that people who are unsaved read this book and devotion series, but not like they would read any other dating/relationship advice book. This book and devotion series is about handling our lives on Earth and our interactions with people of the opposite sex in a way that is pleasing to God. It is about recognizing that no matter what your relationship status happens to be, loving God should be your first priority.

The purpose for our lives is the praise and to please God; to live holy and righteously as a testimony to those who may never read a Bible, but will read our lives. We must set an example of how to love one another and keep God as our first love. This is the ultimate courtship. What we do with the time God gives us on Earth shows Him and those who observe us just how real He is in our lives and how much we love Him. We need to pray that we make the most of our relationship with God, and, if it is His will for us to find or be found by a spouse, that we love that person the way God loves us. Because, there will come a day when the courtship will end and the Church, the Bride of Christ, will be with Him forever. And, I cannot speak for anyone else, but I want the end result of my earthly life to be the beginning of my eternal life as a servant with whom God was pleased.

Prayer

Thank You, God for promising to love us forever.
Please forgive me for living as if the things of this world are all that matter.
Lord, please help me to always love You first regardless what my relationship status happens to be.

In Jesus' Name,
Amen

Reflections for the Week

Read and meditate on this week's Scripture. Say the
prayer at the end of the devotion daily and ask for
God's wisdom. Write down any revelations or
reflections you may have throughout the week.

_____

_____

_____

_____

_____

_____

_____

_____

_____

_____

_____

_____

_____

Made in the USA
Columbia, SC
30 January 2020